T0114274

Praise for *Care of the Soul in Medicine*

*"I wish **Care of the Soul in Medicine** had been available when I was a medical student, because it is one of the wisest guides for health-care professionals I have ever read. Moore shows that without attention to the spirit, there can be no true healing. If taken seriously, the wisdom in his book could transform medicine in America. This book is desperately needed by patients, too, and by all those who love and care for them."*

— **Larry Dossey, M.D.**, author of *The Power of Premonitions* and *Healing Words*

"This accessible and engaging book reminds us that caring is a sacred calling; that care of the body is care of the soul; and that health care practiced with depth, beauty, respect, and meaning can transform our hospitals into temples of healing. I would love to think that every medical student would read this book."

— **Michael Kearney, M.D.**, medical director of palliative care service at Santa Barbara Cottage Hospital, associate medical director at Visiting Nurse and Hospice Care, medical director to the Anam Cara Project for Compassionate Companionship in Life and Death, and author of *Place of Healing* and *Mortally Wounded*

*"Thomas Moore's **Care of the Soul in Medicine** is an unusually thoughtful exploration of current medical culture and its focus on treatment and cure, often at the expense of caring and healing. He makes an inspirational and convincing case for true transformation in health care that goes beyond our fascination with technology to encompass heart, mind, and spirit."*

— **Susan B. Frampton, Ph.D.**, president of Planetree, a nonprofit organization and internationally recognized leader in patient-centered care

CARE OF THE SOUL IN MEDICINE

ALSO BY THOMAS MOORE

The Planets Within
Rituals of the Imagination
A Blue Fire
Dark Eros
Care of the Soul
Meditations
Soul Mates
The Re-Enchantment of Everyday Life
The Education of the Heart
The Book of Job
The Soul of Sex
Original Self
The Soul's Religion
Dark Nights of the Soul
A Life at Work
*Writing in the Sand**
*The Guru of Golf**

*Available from Hay House

Please visit:
Hay House USA: www.hayhouse.com®
Hay House Australia: www.hayhouse.com.au
Hay House UK: www.hayhouse.co.uk
Hay House India: www.hayhouse.co.in

CARE OF THE SOUL IN MEDICINE

Healing Guidance for Patients, Families,
and the People Who Care for Them

THOMAS MOORE

HAY HOUSE, INC.
Carlsbad, California • New York City
London • Sydney • New Delhi

Published in the United States by: Hay House, Inc.: www.hayhouse.com •
Published in Australia by: Hay House Australia Pty. Ltd.: www.hayhouse.
com.au • *Published in the United Kingdom by:* Hay House UK, Ltd.:
www.hayhouse.co.uk • *Published in India by:* Hay House Publishers
India: www.hayhouse.co.in

Design: Tricia Breidenthal

Library of Congress Cataloging-in-Publication Data

Moore, Thomas.
  Care of the soul in medicine : healing guidance for patients,
families, and the people who care for them / Thomas Moore. -- 1st ed.
    p. cm.
  Includes bibliographical references.
  ISBN 978-1-4019-2563-5 (hardcover : alk. paper) 1. Medicine--
Religious aspects. 2. Pastoral medicine. I. Title.
  BL65.M4M65 2010
  201'.661--dc22
                                  2009045961

Tradepaper ISBN: 978-1-4019-2564-2
Digital ISBN: 978-1-4019-2799-8

1st edition, April 2010
2nd edition, July 2011

Printed in the United States of America

Notice how this snake coils around my staff.
Remember exactly what he looks like.
I will change myself into this snake, but
I will be much larger, I will be immense, like
the body of a god who transforms himself.

— ASKLEPIOS, IN OVID'S *METAMORPHOSES*, XV

CONTENTS

PART IV: PATIENT HEALERS

PREFACE

There is a beautiful story in the Acts of Peter and the Twelve Apostles, a Gnostic text, in which Jesus goes by the name Lithargoel. The word breaks down into the Greek words *lithos* (stone) and *argos* (silver), and the Hebrew *el* (angel). Jesus is the shining spirit stone. Around his waist he wears a packet of medicine. He is a healer and promises to give people pearls. But he means himself. He is the pearl. He is the medicine, just as doctors and nurses, and all of us in our healer capacity, are the real medicine.

Buddhists honor a similar healer they call the Lapis Lazuli Radiant Healing Buddha, who holds a bowl of medicine in one hand and a healing plant in the other. He is surrounded by a halo of bright colors. His followers promise to heal with their personal radiance and presence. I think every nurse, doctor, and patient should be a devotee of this Buddha.

These inspiring and colorful images could bring new life to modern medicine, which has gained immensely from its application of the scientific method but has also lost the spiritual radiance of traditional medicine. Along with that radiance has gone some of medicine's soul.

In this book I want to offer some suggestions of how medicine could move into an exciting and much-expanded future. I recommend taking into account the body, soul, and spirit as all being implicated in every illness and therefore having a role in every medical examination and procedure. I put special emphasis on places of healing, pointing in certain deep directions where architecture and furnishing can create an atmosphere in which people feel like complete human beings and in which they are helped in every dimension of their being.

INTRODUCTION

Thirty years ago I was living in a rented house just a block from Southern Methodist University in Dallas when I began practicing psychotherapy. People came into my small, book-lined room there mainly with complaints of the soul: they were depressed or having trouble in marriage or finding it difficult to get life in place. Some came with spiritual issues: they didn't want to live in a body and therefore had trouble with food, or they had been following a guru and had become disillusioned and rootless. In some cases the problem was more physical.

One evening a woman called me and asked to have a special late-night session. She had a bad skin problem and was scheduled for surgery the next morning. She showed up around 9 P.M. and talked about her life situation, especially the problems she was having with her husband and two children. We explored certain patterns that had ruled her life for many years and seemed to lie in the background of her family issues. The next morning she called to say that her skin lesions had disappeared and the surgery was canceled.

This was the most remarkable instance I witnessed where talk cleared up a physical problem, but I have no doubt that life patterns, ways of finding meaning, and long-standing emotional habits lie at the root of physical illnesses and therefore that caring for the soul and spirit could play an essential role in healing them.

This book is not about near-miraculous healings but rather about ways in which the practice of medicine could take into account the psychological, relational, and spiritual aspects of a person going through the rigors of medical treatment. Even if addressing these dimensions didn't cure the illness, it could make the process of healing faster, more complete, and more satisfying. Both health-care professionals and patients could come to medicine with an eye toward healing the whole person and not the body alone.

What Is a Person?

People are among the most obvious and identifiable beings we deal with every day, and yet it isn't easy to say precisely what a person is. In my practice I see people whose world of meaning overlaps with their world of physical pain, and you wonder how one affects the other. Is the body a person? Does illness always affect every aspect of a person? I believe that exploring these questions could lead to a more humane health-care system, one that offers deep emotional meaning and sublime spiritual comfort.

In my practice of psychotherapy I have often seen body and soul interact. Suddenly bereft of meaning, a woman complained of stomach problems and sexual difficulties. A man who was overly sensitive to criticism developed a severe skin disease. Another man who had never been able to express his anger struggled with colitis. A woman who complained of frequent headaches always had, I noticed, deep furrows in her forehead.

I have come to think of body, soul, and spirit as three sides of the triangle that is a whole person, and now I also include relationships—family members, lovers, friends, spouses—as well as work and all kinds of experiences in my definition of a person.

Today medical practitioners speak of treating "the whole person," but the modern idea of personhood is limited. My paradigm offers a comprehensive way to picture a complete person who presents himself at a doctor's office or a hospital. It is a four-dimensional person who is defined by others close to him and by the world in which he lives.

Let me sketch it this way:

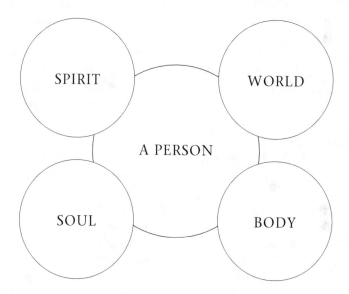

There are moments in doing therapy when I wish I were a physician so I could more precisely tend to the whole person sitting in front of me, doing something specific for his physical pain. I have felt a similar but reverse urge as a patient presenting myself to the health-care system—I wish I could inject some soul and spirit into the medical world.

Body: The Physical Life of the Soul

I'm often invited to speak at conferences that have "mind-body-spirit" in their titles. I don't know how this popular phrase came into existence, but it is lacking, since it leaves out the soul. It may sound like a matter of semantics, but it is much more than that. That which we can't imagine and express in words remains hidden and neglected.

In older philosophies the mind is tucked into the larger category of spirit, part of that urge in us to transcend the material life and our ignorance through knowledge, power, and experience. The deep soul points in a different direction: it is the focus of our humanity and individuality, our emotions and memories, our fears and desires. The soul is especially concerned about those things that make us secure and give us a sense of belonging: home, family, love, place, friends, and work. While the spirit often prefers solitude and detachment, the soul comes alive in community and prefers attachment.

In the history of religious spirituality, detachment has been an important value, and it contributes to a spiritual life. If you can be less concerned about making money, staying close to your family, and having many things in your life, you are free to explore meaning and values and develop a way of life committed to a grand vision. Medicine takes this route when a hospital focuses entirely on curing a patient and disregarding his work life, his family, and the things that are important to him. Hospitals evoke a pure "spirit" atmosphere with white uniforms, colorless and imageless walls, and a general atmosphere of function and activity.

Most people don't use the word "spirit" in this way, so let me explain. Philosophies deriving from Plato distinguish spirit from soul. Spirit is any attempt to go beyond the status quo, the body, and personal limitations. In this sense, education is a spirit activity, and for good reason we speak of "higher education." Soul is down and deep, close to experience, known in feelings and passions and revealed in physical expression and even illness.

A soulful environment might be cluttered with objects of comfort or memories of home, while a more spirited place will focus on getting the job done without frills or human distractions. Soul is known in its variety, and so colors and textures abound. Spirit tends to favor symbols of purity and focus, and so white is a common choice of color. In a hospital, an emphasis on spirit may accentuate technology and procedure over the personal needs of a patient.

One day I sat with a patient, Ira, in his hospital room while he was being examined by a series of nurses. He had a slightly sardonic sense of humor that he expressed constantly. Rarely did he give the nurses a straight answer. He had lymphatic cancer and now lung cancer, but this day the nurses were concerned about his irregular heartbeat. They checked his blood pressure continually and looked at readouts on an EKG machine at the foot of his bed. They didn't say what they thought was wrong. They looked nervous, and their constant assurances didn't persuade either of us.

Finally Ira asked them, "What do you see there?" He was referring to the EKG printouts. A friendly and caring nurse said, "Your heartbeat is abnormal." When she used that word, my ears pricked up. I remembered a cardiologist once saying that about me. "Abnormal?" Ira shouted. "You're telling me I'm abnormal?"

The nurses left to seek out a cardiologist, upping the ante for Ira, of course. He became more anxious. "I want to get out of this hospital as soon as I can," he said to the next nurse who came into the room.

"What do you like least about it?" I asked him.

He spread his arms out and pointed to the small, cluttered room. "I have nothing to do," he said.

"What is your work?" I asked. I didn't put it in the past

tense, because people often don't want to think about illness taking away their work lives.

"I used to be a pipe fitter," he said. "One day I fell and then got weak. I couldn't go back to the job. The worst thing about being sick is that I don't bring in the $60,000 I used to make. My wife is worried. I feel bad."

This man, lying in a bed with tubes and wires streaming from his body, missed his world and was concerned about his family.

If medicine were to grant more attention to the soul, it would see the importance of beautiful things, the people in a patient's life, and the loss he may feel in being held in a place so focused on cure. A more soul-centered medical practice would respect attachments of all kinds and understand the importance of things like familiar food and a more homelike environment. Maybe it could even design a hospital stay in which a patient might be able to get something done in his world. I know that for me, concern for my family and the itch to do my work would be overwhelming.

In this book I want to address both health professionals and patients. I want to explore ways to make a hospital or a doctor's office soulful and spiritual. I also want to show patients how they might care for their soul and spirit as they navigate a materialistic health-care system. When a person gets sick, everything in that patient's being is affected but only a small portion is addressed.

Later I will spell out what I mean by soul. For now, just know that I am not referring to an object of religious belief or some spiritual entity out there in the ether. My work does not derive from any particular religious belief system or from any New Age approach to healing. We commonly talk about music having soul, about soul food, a soulful person, a house with soul. Essentially that is what I mean by the word, though I can get more technical.

For some, the word *healing* could be a problem, too. It may sound sentimental, magical, and inflated, but I don't mean it that way. I am simply referring to the aim of every health-care worker to cure disease, manage injury, ease pain, rehabilitate, and offer comfort. Etymologically, "heal" comes from "whole"; it means to put back together what has been broken apart—bones, organs, health, normal life at home and at work, emotional calm, and important relationships.

Why do I include "world" in the diagram of what a person is? Because we are defined as much by the world around us as by our inner experience. You see a patient lying in a hospital bed and think that his illness is all there on the bed. But if you could crawl into his head, you would find concerns about the family, the house, the neighborhood, work, the car, perhaps even international politics. They are not only a big part of the patient's experience; they may be at least partly the cause of his sickness.

Concretely we know that poisons in the air and water and in the objects we use can make us seriously ill. Many are carcinogenic, and yet, thinking about illness as an inside-body affair, medicine doesn't take the lead in cleaning up the toxic environment. It keeps treating individual patients as though the world has nothing to do with illness and has no role in its cure. It acts as though the world isn't sick, though we all know that the opposite is true.

I remember visiting my mother when she was just entering the phase of dementia after a serious stroke. She walked to the window of her little room, looked out, and spoke with considerable longing. "I'd like to be home," she said.

Then she asked me if the street she was looking at was just down from her house. She was quite sure it was. She was looking for signs of the neighbors. In fact, she was about four or five miles away in an area she didn't know well. It was sad for me to sense her longing for home, knowing that we couldn't take care of her there. She had the look and sound of someone whose mind had been affected by the stroke, but I felt this wasn't about confusion. Her imagination was taking her home, and, as in a dream, she was there at some level.

I encouraged her to talk about home, since it was so much on her mind. When she did, she seemed to let it go, at least for a while. But there was no doubt that her house, her things, and her neighbors were part of her life, part of who she was. We don't seem to appreciate the shock to people snatched out of their familiar worlds and resettled in strange hospital rooms and unfamiliar beds. But this loss of world may well get in the way of healing, especially when health-care workers are unconscious of it and unaware of its importance.

We are also insensitive to the new reality of a hospital, with its institutional architecture, staff, and equipment. Nurses and housekeeping attendants replace the neighbors. A patient gets to know them the way you know your neighbors—they are not intimately connected, but they see each other several times a day. They establish a relationship. Care for that new world is a crucial element in the healing process.

A New Vision for Medicine

Medicine today appears to fit snugly in the age of science. We treat the body as an object unrelated to emotion and meaning and spiritual power. We deal with organs and body parts as separate entities unrelated to the whole. We not only train doctors in science; we enculturate them, make them see the body as an object, and require them to honor the scientific method and be wary of any alternatives. We measure advances in medicine largely by the sophistication of the machines we introduce into a hospital and by new research in pharmacology. In our doctors we admire professionalism, competence, and objectivity.

This exclusive emphasis on the scientific and technological practice of medicine is relatively new. Just 400 years ago, one of the famous doctors in England, Robert Fludd, who studied at Oxford and on the Continent in the years around 1600, was an alchemist, wrote a book on the profound connection between macrocosm (the universe) and microcosm (the human being), and used music as his main metaphor and template for treatment.

Four hundred years is not so long ago. My father is now 96. If his fathers before him lived similarly long lives, my great-great-grandfather would have been alive when Dr. Fludd was studying medicine and experimenting with a salve, formulated through alchemy, to be used in warfare by putting it on the weapon that caused a wound.

Shamans and other spiritual leaders have the role of healer and doctor in their communities and are often remarkably effective in dealing with wounds and illnesses. Prayer, ritual, meditation, and music have the power to heal, and yet we don't use them seriously and widely in medical practice because they lie outside the paradigm, the myth, and the accepted story of modern medicine.

My teenage daughter, who suffers from Hashimoto's disease, an autoimmune illness that attacks the thyroid, sometimes goes to see a healer, Guru Dev, who has been a shaman and now practices within the Sikh tradition. He holds her hand and meditates and "sees" what is going on with her body. She trusts him and feels beneficial changes in her body—she rubs her belly and says "something shifted me"—after a meeting with him.

Once, I had a session with him that had a small but important impact on me. My wife, my daughter, and I went to an ashram that Guru Dev, who travels around the world healing and teaching, was visiting in our area of New England. The session was to be for me and Siobhán, who was 16 at the time. We all agreed that she and I would have a half hour each with Guru Dev.

Siobhán began. The healer held her hand and they sat quietly on the floor in the corner of the room. I sat nearby and watched quietly. After what seemed to be three minutes, he let go of her hand and motioned for me to join him. I leaned over to my wife and whispered, "I thought we were to have a half hour each. Siobhán has had only two or three minutes."

"What do you mean?" my wife whispered back. "She's been with him for almost an hour."

I don't know how time got compressed. It didn't feel like a simple, everyday occurrence of time going by quickly. I was jolted by the information that so much time had passed. After I had sat with Guru Dev for my turn, he recommended the yoga "breath of fire" and told me that with a little practice I could tell how the blood was flowing through my heart vessels. I came away with a different way of seeing my body, with an intimacy with my physical being I hadn't had before. The slippage in time, not terribly significant in itself, taught me to think of healing as taking place in an altered state.

I am a fairly normal person from a working-class neighborhood in Detroit. My father was a plumber, as was the majority of men in our family. I don't visit healers often or practice yoga regularly or have a taste for New Age practices. I have submitted to standard medical expertise for tonsillectomy, appendectomy, and angioplasty. I take several pills each day for high blood pressure, cholesterol, and thyroid.

But for all its advances, I see severe limitations in modern medicine. I'm alive because of the wondrous technology of angioplasties and stents. I'm healthy because of easy access to drugs. I profoundly appreciate how far scientific medicine has come in the last hundred years, but I'm also acutely aware of how limited its vision is.

I see widespread arrogance among doctors, especially surgeons and other specialists. I see patients being treated badly and too quickly. I see hospitals that feel like body factories rather than places of healing. I see families of seriously ill and dying people merely tolerated, rather than welcomed, wandering the halls of hospitals and making endless telephone calls trying to get some life-and-death information about a loved one.

I hear of doctors dispensing antidepressants as cure-alls for any sign of emotional weakness. I hear of them offering platitudes and truisms when spiritual and emotional guidance is called for. Mostly, I hear of them having no time or taste for "superstitious" extravagances that challenge or even just nudge the beloved machinery and chemistry of modern healing.

I remember my dear Aunt Helen anxiously going from doctor to doctor to try to find out the cause of strong heart palpitations. She found out too late that she had a large tumor pressing against her chest, and she died not long after her discovery. One day I looked into her eyes and saw such anxiety that it broke my heart. This good woman knew that there was something seriously wrong with her, but she couldn't find a doctor to take care of her. Looking at her distress, I knew that there was something wrong with our medical system.

I remember my mother's case. She was at our small cottage on Lake Huron with her sister, my Aunt Betty, when she started to choke on a peanut. My aunt recognized the signs of a stroke and took her immediately to the nearest hospital. They checked my mother over and dismissed her. The next day she had another, bigger attack and was hospitalized in Detroit. I spoke with her on the telephone that night and I remember her telling me how good the doctors and nurses were to her. The next day she had a brain hemorrhage, which marked the beginning of her descent toward death.

In the next few weeks our family was desperate to find out if the doctors thought she could survive the stroke. We tried to ask her attending physician but were told that we would have to find her at the hospital between 6 and 8 A.M., when she did her rounds—an impossible challenge for us.

Otherwise, we'd be kept in the dark. I couldn't believe the insensitivity to a family so concerned about their very dear and precious mother.

Wonderful, heroic, and heartfelt deeds take place in hospitals every day, and doctors and nurses give themselves unselfishly during long and difficult hours of work. Still, the medical system is a beast to tangle with and there are an equal number of stories of emotional brutality and insensitivity.

Theoretically we know that emotional attention and a vision about healing can help people survive and thrive during illness, but the medical world doesn't always put its action where its research is. It glides over the basic needs of patients to be listened to, comforted, and inspired. It trains its eyes on its numbers and machinery and fails to see the need for a conversation, for tender guidance and spiritual inspiration.

This book is about medicine treating the whole person and not just an organ or a body part. It considers what a whole person is: body, soul, spirit, and that person's world. It re-visions medicine as a means of dealing with sickness by attending to the spiritual, emotional, relational, and physical needs of a patient. It imagines what a hospital might look like if it envisioned a whole person and understood the meaning of the phrase *healing environment.* It explores the calling of healers and tries to help patients navigate the medical world so as to be healed in their whole being.

The Body Imagined as a Machine

The 20th century, which still has us in its grip, was a time devoted to scientific information and technological evolution. It truly accomplished miracles, and I have no doubt that much-esteemed visionaries of the past, like Robert Fludd, would have given anything to see an MRI machine or a heart transplant. But for all its achievements, the 20th century didn't help us raise children well; deal with violence in our homes, in our streets, or among nations; or make a more beautiful and harmonious society. We built machines and ignored the human issues.

This philosophy that compares a human being to a machine stretches back at least to 18th-century images of the human being as a complicated clock, and it applies to medicine. Our achievements have been extraordinary but one-dimensional. I foresee the 21st century expanding our vision. I expect that in medicine we will learn much more about the impact upon our health of specific emotions and experiences and worlds of meaning. We will learn to deal generously and seriously with families, with our healing environments, with the complete education of doctors and nurses, with ways to bring spiritual vision and methods to healing, and with the basic human needs of people in distress over a bad turn in their health and well-being.

This book is a kind of manifesto, written by someone who is a reflective patient and not a physician or medical researcher. It's a wake-up call and an initial charting of a new, all-embracing approach to medicine. It is not a grand detour into some New Age and esoteric kind of "healing," but a close examination of medicine as it is practiced today, with suggestions from a layman for how it could expand and embrace the whole person.

There can be no doubt now that there is a serious movement in our culture toward a new way of being. In all areas, including medicine, old philosophies are breaking up and a new vision is falling into place. Religious institutions are facing the challenge of a more personal and immediate spirituality. In the United States, a black man and a woman competed for the presidency of the country, and the black man became president.

The turn of a century, to say nothing of a millennium, invites us to rethink where we have arrived and what we're doing here. This is a good time—this year, this decade—to imagine a different future for medicine. This is the time to move in a new direction and not merely expand on the old one. This is the time for us all to become healers of persons rather than technicians of the body.

PART I

BODY
AND SOUL

*One could call every illness
an illness of the soul.*

— NOVALIS

CHAPTER 1

CARING
FOR PEOPLE,
NOT JUST
BODIES

Just a few months after *Care of the Soul* was published in 1992, I received a call from Dr. Steven Duane at the Park Nicollet Cancer Center in Minneapolis, asking me to consult for his staff and give some talks. As an experienced psychotherapist, I had long been interested in healing of all kinds, but I had never considered my work as directly relevant to medicine. I felt a bit intimidated, but the challenge excited me, and so I went.

I found the staff at that time competent in their various roles and specialties and the director a true visionary and humanitarian. But I could feel at the first encounter that they were under unusual strain. They were welcoming to me and yet reserved, obviously reticent to talk about any conflicts at the center, but eventually the story came out.

These highly skilled and giving people had had excellent educations in the science of medicine, but they found it difficult to deal with the frequent deaths among their patients. They were academically and clinically skilled and confident, but emotionally and spiritually less well trained. I would find over the following years that this is the case for many medical caregivers: They are competent technicians but often uncertain about how to deal with tragic news, distraught families, and patients facing their mortality. Sometimes they simply burn out from the emotional drain of dealing with patients and families in distress.

Some staff members at Park Nicollet in that year were also troubled by a trend among their patients to pursue what was then called "alternative medicine." Acupuncture, massage, vitamins, unusual diets—people with nothing to lose and desperate for any promise of cure complemented their care at Park Nicollet with visits to herbalists and practitioners of traditional Chinese medicine. The staff was concerned that their patients were either wasting their time and money or exposing themselves to dangerous methods. Times have changed and today most medical centers make an effort to include "alternative," "complementary," or "integrative" approaches.

Integrative medicine is a natural doorway for letting soul and spirit into the medical world. Massage, diet, hypnosis, meditation, yoga, and acupuncture presuppose a whole person. They ask that we consider pleasure, relaxation, and spiritual practice as implicated in illness and health. At Park Nicollet, I felt that the staff just needed to express their concerns instead of keeping them private.

Patient and Family in Treatment

Dr. Duane asked me to speak one evening to a large gathering of cancer patients and their families, and it was then that I began to learn from patients and families how health care needs to change. I knew from years of study that the human soul has a profound need for home and family. I also knew that the soul has thin and porous borders. A person's soul bleeds over into the soul of the marriage, the family, the neighborhood, and so on. When a person gets sick, the whole family feels the affliction.

Modern medicine tends to think of illness as belonging to the individual's body. Families, it assumes, are of course concerned about the sick person, but they are on a tangent, not part of the problem. Even in enlightened hospitals, families often get crumbs of attention, space, and time, and this is because we see illness as a problem of the body, not of the entire person, especially not of other people who lie within a patient's intimate boundaries.

The auditorium that night was filled with family members who were intent on helping their loved ones because they knew that a patient in a hospital needs a dedicated advocate and navigator. Nowhere more than in a hospital does the squeaky wheel get attention. Nowhere does a person, removed from the familiar territory of home and work, weakened by illness, and inferior in knowledge and skill, have more need for a family member willing to speak loudly out of love and care.

I returned from Minnesota with deep admiration for what Dr. Duane and his staff were doing and with a few key ideas about medicine in mind: the emotional needs and skills among caregivers, the role of families in illness and treatment, and the need to expand our vision in medicine beyond what hard science can offer. Today Dr. Duane says this about his work: "I have a deep respect for the impact that cancer has on a person, both physically and emotionally. I try to incorporate that respect into my practice of oncology." Albert Schweitzer was guided by one principle in his outstanding service—reverence for life. I feel slightly closer to Dr. Duane's principle—respect for the person.

When I came home from Park Nicollet I felt motivated to learn more about health care and come up with ways of restoring its soul. I was on alert, then, when other medical establishments invited me to speak at conferences, medical schools, hospices, and hospitals.

Symbolic Gestures

Next in line was Memorial Sloan-Kettering Cancer Center in New York. This was a large conference on cancer at which many researchers and physicians spoke. I sat in the auditorium watching one expert after another show slides of charts and percentages and procedures, each one using laser pointers and skilled with the current state of slide projection and obviously competent in his or her specialty.

When it was my turn, I stood up and spoke without any charts or pointers and focused my attention on simple things: the low-cost, low-tech changes that would add the dimension of soul to the practice of medicine. My book was popular at the time, so people listened. I told them of the human need for home—not the literal place necessarily, but the spirit of home. I discussed memory, storytelling, dreams, and food—items that form the substance of this book.

I had the impression, as I spoke, that my simple language was a bit out of place at this conference that valued the quantification of experience, but in the discussion period a woman stood to support my emphasis on the little, human aspects of treatment and care. She told of a patient in her hospice who was on the verge of dying. She asked him if there was anything she could do for him in his last hours. "I'd like some banana bread," he said. So she went home and baked a loaf of banana bread for him and thought it was the most soulful thing she could do. He died peacefully and happily with this symbol of his former, happy life at home.

I learned at Sloan-Kettering that hospice workers were way ahead of me in sorting out the human needs of the seriously ill. They knew from intimate experiences with the dying what was important in the end. I loved the story of the banana bread, not only because I could well make the same request, but because this caregiver knew that food could be an effective way of bringing soul to medical care. I didn't overlook the suggestion, in the story, of a homespun kind of communion rite in the man's request.

We'll consider food later, especially how hospitals might rethink their notions of diet and nutrition. Food has highly symbolic value for the human soul and means far more than calories and fat content. But this story goes beyond food as nourishment. It reminds us to be aware of the deep-seated symbolic value of simple things to patients dealing head-on with their mortality.

Sloan-Kettering put me in a hot seat between the immensely impressive knowledge and skills of modern medicine and the simpler needs of people when they are sick. It reminded me of my studies in religion, where I learned to see spiritual forms in ordinary situations— communion with home-baked banana bread. It encouraged me to bring my own vision of the soul, the simple life, and symbolic experience into any and all modern medical settings. I knew that I was in for a big challenge.

An Awareness of Suffering

Many medical conferences and visits to medical institutions followed over the years, including an invitation to speak at the University of Tennessee College of Medicine in Knoxville. There I had experiences that helped me understand health care from the inside.

I remember the first time I spoke at this medical center. The day began early with surgeons in attendance. After the talk, as people were gathering around me, two or three surgeons handed me notes asking if I would join them in the operating rooms to see what it was like to be a surgeon. I took these invitations as poignant expressions of their desire to add the element of soul to their practice.

Later, everywhere I went I was told that surgeons are a breed apart, people so highly educated in the methods of science that they usually have little patience for the "soft" matters like family, the healing milieu, and the arts. Yet some surgeons handle their calling in a different way. Their proximity to death and the power in their hands bring them to consider the ultimate issues, and they are drawn to spiritual matters and to the arts.

Dr. Allan J. Hamilton writes:

> No one told me you couldn't undertake major surgery—as patient or doctor—without opening yourself up to spiritual realignment and, sometimes, outright transformation. . . . Every patient steers me closer to my soul's purpose.[1]

Some doctors I interviewed clung defensively to their modernism, the faith in science and technical skill. They were not free to explore the matters of soul and spirit, which they judged to be naïve and ignorant. My guess is that they never had the chance to learn about the intelligence in ancient philosophy or modern art. They could see only two opposed categories—science and superstition.

One time at Tennessee a small group of doctors were disturbed by what I was saying. They interpreted me to be criticizing science and challenging the bedrock of their medical philosophy, the scientific, objective view of the body. They invited me to a small, windowless room and asked me to sit at the end of a narrow, laminated conference table. One doctor produced a typed list of objections he had to my message, concluding that, contrary to my description of illness as a mystery to be heard and respected, illness is a problem to be solved. "Within 20 years," he said with an edge to his voice, "medicine will have solved all mysteries."

I was sitting there noticing the doctors' starched shirts and expensive jackets and perfectly knotted ties—everything too perfect and neat for my comfort. But I didn't feel threatened or worried, and I didn't modify my message. I felt that the doctors who created this mini-inquisition could not look from a distance at the myth that had them in its grip. They were relating to the paradigm of scientific medicine as though it was a religion, they the prime believers and its priests, and apparently they felt a strong need to defend it.

My host in Knoxville, Rev. George Doebler, was a Lutheran minister, a deceptively plain-talking, no-nonsense, big-hearted man who had created a large and flourishing program in pastoral care. I've known George for almost ten years now and have never seen a man so easygoing and yet so devoted to the job of caring for the souls of hospital patients.

One thing I noticed in my visits to the University of Tennessee Medical Center was the impact George, Steve, and their staff have had on the huge hospital. They have the respect of people in all areas of health care and create an atmosphere in the hospital far beyond what their numbers might ordinarily allow. Here is an important lesson: because the emotional and spiritual aspects of health care often go unnoticed, when chaplains do their work well, they teach by example and create a healing environment through their sheer presence.

If a person follows his or her genius and stands up to the establishment, eventually others, if not the entire institution, may come around and appreciate what that person is doing. We all want to do our jobs well. We don't want to be ignorant or behind the times. But we have our prejudices. Seeing someone working successfully in a way we might normally disapprove of, we change and learn new ways of thinking.

When I teach doctors and psychotherapists on Cape Cod in summer sessions, I show them a set of Buddhist vows ascribed to the Lapis Lazuli Radiant Healing Buddha. One of them says, "I will heal by my radiance and my presence."[2] I wish all health-care workers had this vow written somewhere on the walls of their offices. You are always going to radiate some attitude or message; you may as well radiate the best you have.

One day, on a visit to Knoxville, George and I were walking through the hallways of the hospital when he noticed a woman on a gurney with her arm stretched out as though in desperation. She was mumbling unintelligible sounds and looked as though she might fall off the gurney. Without losing a stride, George went over and talked to her. "She's schizophrenic," he told me when he rejoined me. "Why the hell isn't someone taking care of her?"

Chaplains used to take care of their own, the people who believed as they did and were members of their religion. Today, in many places the chaplain is available to all. Certainly a Catholic or Jewish or Lutheran chaplain will respond to someone of his or her tradition, but generally they are there in the hospital for anyone who needs them. In today's jargon, you could say that as counselors they are often more spiritual than religious.

George's quick-thinking and spontaneous response to the woman on the gurney made a deep impression on me. This is what pastoral counselors should be about. They should be offering solace to the most neglected and doing it without respect to belief or creed or race. They should be radiating a spirit of care and attention.

Conversation as Care

Knowing that these soul issues play an integral role in illness and healing, health-care workers at every level could engage patients in conversation. You don't have to have any special goals. You just listen and talk. The mind gains a great deal from information and lecture; the soul gains more from mere conversation, the simple human act of talking about whatever comes to mind.

Nurses and doctors sometimes worry about their professionalism. They understand that authority has a place in delivering health care effectively. But it is possible to do both at the same time: present yourself as a professional and be a human being. A nurse or doctor should also know that a simple conversation is a soulful act and is far more significant than it might appear.

An easy entry into conversation is not easy for some people. Some doctors become eloquent when reciting research findings but stammer and grope when having a simple conversation. Certain professionals could benefit from a few lessons in this simple act.

A first step, in this important if mundane act of conversation, is to receive what a person has to say. Let the patient set the agenda. Don't be impatient; stop and listen. The patient's words may sound trite and commonplace, but if you listen closely you may well hear a significant theme in what the patient says. Or you may detect a strong emotion.

The second step is to encourage talk about those things that matter—home, family, and the rest—and see what corresponds to the patient's actual concern. Patients are often more worried about family members than about themselves. A nurse or doctor could help relieve these worries through a few well-chosen words.

It's difficult to convey the importance of soul care because it is such a simple practice. You speak casually with people about ordinary things. You prepare good food for friends. You keep your home respectable and comfortable. You raise your children to be thoughtful and caring people. You love without fear or anxiety.

Medical professionals go through a highly demanding education, sorting through the complexities of the body, medical procedures, and pharmacology. Understandably, they may feel that they have no time for simple things like conversation and family dynamics. Technical issues appear to be more urgent than the human ones.

Once, when I was a professor at a large university, feeling misunderstood by my colleagues because of my interest in the soul, my friend James Hillman advised me. "In that setting, the soul is going to lose," he said. His words burned into me, because I was already sensing excitement among my students and judgment from my colleagues. A few years later, the university denied me tenure.

Some of those feelings come back to me now when I visit hospitals and medical schools. Generally, the nurses are eager to talk about soul issues, while the doctors have more important things on their minds. On the other hand, some doctors show curiosity about the soul, often thinking that they are lacking some key insight, the way a person enters therapy—they know they have troubling feelings that need attention, but they don't want to show weakness.

The Soul's Psychology

This book is full of ideas about how to be a soulful doctor, nurse, or other medical caregiver and how to be a soulful patient as well. But there is one issue that stands out above all others affecting the important relationship between medical professional and patient. To be a soulful person you have to have made some progress toward dealing with your own psychological issues. If a doctor is insecure in her knowledge, she may bring that insecurity into her relationship to patients through arrogance and emotional distance. If a nurse has an overwhelming need to help people, he may act out that personal need in an overbearing and perhaps smothering kind of care.

I was once speaking to a group of nurses who had gathered for a luncheon conversation and brought up the mother complex. A complex is a group of emotions, ideas, and memories focused around a particular theme. We operate out of complexes every day, and usually they can be beneficial. But frequently they get out of hand. For instance, most people understand an inferiority complex. Some people feel worthless and incapable so profoundly that no matter what you say to give them confidence, they keep sinking in their own estimation of themselves. In long and deep conversation a psychotherapist can glimpse the roots of the complex and, over time, help ease its burden. But usually it harms relationships and gets in the way of good work.

The medical world naturally attracts many people with mother complexes. That day when I was speaking to the nurses, I asked them how many of them were aware of a mother complex at work in their own calling. They all laughed, because they knew that the maternal spirit was everywhere in the nursing profession. The complex has the positive effect of bringing people into nursing and helping them endure long, difficult workdays. But it can also get in the way. Nurses can go too far in offering comfort and care.

Any complex has a bright side and a shadow side. The shadow of the mother might be control, judgment, a punishing attitude, withdrawal of affection, and treating adults as children. I once went to a dentist whose assistant had such a strong mother complex—she talked to me as if I were a toddler—that I quit after one visit. I have a strong mother figure in me, and I don't tolerate the same thing too well in others.

The mother is only one of thousands of figures at the core of complexes that get in the way of good medical practice. I've known several doctors who seem to have an "I-am-the-expert" complex. They walk into a room and tell you with their posture and manner that they have had extensive and rigorous medical training and know infinitely more than you do and have no time for small talk and are always in a hurry because so many people need them. Most of this may be true, but it has formed into a psychological complex that sucks the humanity out of their interactions. Patients don't get nearly as much from this competent person as they could if the complex were not so strong.

We all have complexes that get out of hand, and we have to face them and whittle them down to be manageable. We psychotherapists usually have to undergo analysis ourselves for this purpose. Medical professionals, too, could use some form of analysis or personal psychological education to learn how to deal with their complexes.

The Basics of Applied Psychology

This idea of the emotional complex is rich and useful, and it wouldn't be difficult to teach health-care workers to understand their complexes and deal with them. Visit a hospital any day of the week and you will see complexes in action, perhaps more dramatically than in any other venue. Illness and treatment seem to accentuate the unconscious factors that simmer in hearts and minds.

How exactly do you deal effectively with a complex? Let me list a few steps that help defuse a bothersome and potent complex.

1. *Discover what your complexes are.* Everyone has his or her own set of complexes, accounting for personality and struggle. Everyone also has his or her own kind of mother complex and expert complex. You have to recognize your own particular deep issues.

2. *Acknowledge your complex.* The Twelve Step programs are widely known for asking a person to stand up and say, "I am an alcoholic." There is power and effectiveness in a simple declaration of what particular complex has you in its grip. "I am a perpetually mothering person." "I am an overbearing expert."

3. *Don't feed your complex.* I picked up this formula when I was a neophyte psychotherapist in Dallas, probably from Dr. Patricia Berry or James Hillman. When you are about to surrender to a complex, you can decide then and there not to give it anything. One of the most effective ways, once you realize you are about to descend, is to hold your tongue. Don't say the words that are about to come out. Or walk away, if necessary. Find some better expression.

4. *Trace your complex's roots.* The point here is not to explain or blame but simply to tell the history of your complex. You get to know it: how it is special to you, how it may have originated and flowered, and how it has played a role in your life.

5. *Don't get rid of your complex, but fulfill it.* This may sound like paradoxical advice. I get this idea, too, from Dr. Berry, who says that our complexes take us eventually where we need to go. They point in a good direction, even if they are bothersome in their current neurotic form. I now think of a complex as raw material in need of refinement. For example, I consider the title of my book *Care of the Soul* as a positive expression of my own mother complex.

Our educational system is lacking in that it doesn't give us simple psychological knowledge for dealing with items like complexes that interfere with the quality of our work. I'd like to see medical students get a very short course on dealing with their personal issues insofar as they affect their work.

Medicine as Care of the Soul

The soul of medicine is wide in scope. It entails a real engagement of patient and caregiver, a physical environment that promotes health and healing, effective dealing with emotional and personality issues, a sense of calling, presence, a multidimensional view of what a person is, and the capacity to address spiritual issues of meaning, anxiety, vision, hope, and comfort.

You may wonder: Who can possibly fulfill such a calling? Where could a medical student find time to study psychological counseling and the world's religious and spiritual traditions while acquiring the necessary technical knowledge that is constantly expanding? Two aspects of this problem mitigate its difficulty: One, it doesn't take much effort or time to become adequately prepared to deal with soul and spirit. Two, the rewards of being fully present and dealing with whole persons are so much greater than those of the purely physical approach.

There are a few side benefits as well. For example, a human being can't divide his life into compartments, so that he is emotionally defended and distant at work and warm and intimate at home. As the medical worker cares for the whole person on the job, his home life will benefit. In addition, attention to soul and spirit gives the practice of medicine a grander context and a bigger vision. It is easier and more fulfilling to be a person of great vision than to focus only on specific skills and physical issues. I am convinced that dissatisfaction with work in the medical field is largely due to a narrowing of vision.

A patient, too, cannot deal with the full scope of his illness if he focuses only on the physical dimension. The rest of the experience will remain unconscious and therefore not sufficiently addressed. It will linger in the background, causing many problems of relationship and an intense anxiety about the meaning and implications of the problem. Treating soul and spirit in distress eases anxiety, helps relationships, and offers a sense of meaning and hope that will otherwise be elusive.

CHAPTER 2

THE BODY
IS THE SOUL

A few short lines from the poetry of William Blake, the English visionary who single-handedly countered the dehumanizing impact of the industrial/scientific/rationalistic revolution just taking root in his time, will guide us throughout this book:

> Man has no Body distinct from his Soul; for that call'd Body is a portion of Soul discern'd by the five Senses, the chief inlets of Soul in this age.

The soul is the body. The body is the soul. The body is not a slice of meat. It is not a collection of organs, bones, and vessels. The brain is not a computer, and the heart is not just a pump. The body and all its parts are the soul, part of the life of emotion, relationship, and meaning common to us all while we are alive. I'm not able to know what the body and the soul are after death.

Almost 20 years ago, when *Care of the Soul* was first published and I traveled often to speak about it, people would say to me, "Your batteries must be wearing down." I would say, "I have no batteries. The metaphor doesn't sit well with me."

I didn't appreciate the mechanical images for life in a body. Today people talk about the brain as a computer and the whole of the body as wonderful machine. I prefer Aristotle's statement that there are many souls throughout the body. Each organ, each body part, and each cell has a soul, giving it meaning and poetical resonance.

A few years ago I was on a book tour in San Francisco, walking the steep hills as I always do when visiting that beautiful city, when I felt unfamiliar pains in my back. I thought I might have pneumonia, an illness that I have had before on demanding book tours. But when I got home and had put off seeing my doctor for a few weeks, I did a stress test that indicated I could have blockage in an artery. The cardiologist scheduled an angiogram. At one point he invited my wife and daughter into the cath lab to look at the X-rays of my heart and notice the place of the blockage, the left anterior descending artery, sometimes known as the "widow-maker." My daughter was not happy when some blood shot up out of my femoral artery, where they had inserted the probe, but my wife was more aware of the doctor's words. He pointed to the desiccated vessel and said, "His heart is broken." I have since learned that doctors sometime use the expression for a blocked artery, but of course my wife heard the phrase as describing my emotional state.

I don't think my blocked artery represented a "broken heart" at that moment. I was happy in marriage, my home, and my work, and with my children. But I have had many wounds to the heart over the years, beginning with the day I was forced to go to school in first grade when I was five. That was the day I left the Eden of my blissful early childhood, the unbroken company of my adored mother, and the comfort of being at home all day long.

Later, at age 13, I felt a strong urge to go away from home to study for the Catholic priesthood, and I remember another day of parting. I got up at 5 A.M. on a dark September morning. My luggage was packed and a new, long footlocker was ready to be loaded on the train that would take me to Chicago from my home in Detroit. I felt so surreally in shock, in spite of my desire to explore my future, that I thought I might faint. The parting at the train station, where my beloved grandparents and uncles and aunts and cousins had gathered, was exciting but exquisitely painful. And then, for the next 13 years, continuously I felt a wound in my heart from the loss of my family. At the end of every Christmas holiday and summer vacation, I had to make another parting.

All of this may sound melodramatic and childish. These experiences were more complicated than I have described. But from the point of view of my heart, they were intense. I was so homesick at the seminary that I felt physical soreness in my chest.

If I were writing a full biography of my heart, I could describe wounds that stemmed from relationships lost and betrayed. I could tell of careers interrupted, of misunderstandings at work and at home, and of criticisms of my work that cut deeply.

We all have heartaches, some far more upsetting than the ones I have described, and we don't all have heart attacks. I am simply following the signs of my symptoms and noting how they seem to summarize the life of a perhaps overly sensitive person.

"He has a broken heart," the cardiologist said in my 64th year, and I was moved to survey my life for all the moments, some too private to recount here, when my heart was pierced. Saying that, I'm reminded of the central image of the religious order I entered as a young man, the Servites: servants of Mary, the mother of Jesus, a mother who endured so much suffering because of the tragic life of her son that devotional artists pictured her heart pierced by seven swords.

I offer these reflections on a broken heart as an example of what any patient might do in response to any physical illness or disease. You aren't out to prove conclusively what caused the illness but to explore how the body is the soul showing itself in its sad and painful moments. You don't consider the body as an object disconnected from life but rather as the soul impressing itself on your senses.

What Is the Soul?

This book is about how medicine could become more soulful, but it isn't easy to say what the soul is. The word is used in many different ways, sometimes even synonymous with "spirit." I use the word as I find it in the work of James Hillman, the archetypal psychologist. He borrows from C. G. Jung, and Jung followed an ancient tradition that can be traced back to Plotinus, a 3rd-century philosopher who wrote a famous 54-treatise work on the soul entitled *Enneads*. So my special use of the word goes back a long way.

We are all made up of body, soul, and spirit—each element distinct but not separate. The body is Blake's body, the soul perceived by the senses, expressive of emotion and meaning. The spirit is that transcending element in anyone aspiring to a better life, greater understanding, or more inspiring vision. The spirit accounts for religion, meditation, education, and the kind of creativity that moves us into a better future. Steeples, ladders, stairways, night skies, high pulpits, skyscrapers, and rockets all symbolize the spirit's hope for transcendence, to blast away from present limitations.

The soul, in contrast, is grounded in everyday life—home, family, friends, work, food, beauty, nature. Aristotle said that the soul is what makes a thing (or a person) exactly what it is. What makes an axe an axe, he said, is its soul. What makes me what I am essentially, what gives me my deepest identity, is my soul.

The soul is also the depth of a thing or a person. Hillman often quotes the Greek philosopher Herakleitos, who said, "You could never discover the limits of the soul, no matter how many roads you took, so deep is its mystery." *Deep* is a word associated with soul. *Lofty* and *high* are associated with spirit. Thus we get "higher education" and "deep emotions."

If you are looking for your soul, look deep into any aspect of your life. Go down into it: deep into memory, deep into feelings, into your deepest thoughts. There the soul is like a spring from which life pours out.

Mind is part of the life of spirit. The mind appreciates clear logic, information, orderly thinking, research, proofs, and definitions. The soul is different. It prefers poetry and art, insight, reflection, nuance, layers of meaning, mystery, and imagination. Both are valuable and necessary, but they are different in their goals and methods.

Therefore, when we inquire into the soul of medicine, we are looking at illness and treatment, medical practice, and even buildings with deep reflection. We wonder about the poetry in our medical language and images. We are concerned about the experience a patient or a nurse or doctor has in dealing with illness. We are examining not only the function of a tool, a word, or a medical building but also its nuances, its symbolic meanings, and the emotional and poetic impact it has on people.

It may surprise you to hear the word *poetic* used in connection with medicine. We are accustomed to linking medicine with fact. But once you add soul, you are in the realm of meaning and mystery, where facts are not so impressive and where a poetic sensibility leads to your goal. Why is a patient nervous when he is being shuttled into a massive imaging machine? Clearly it is the image of the machine. Who wants to be swallowed by a mechanical device big enough to crush you? You may know that the machine is safe, but the experience of it, its deep symbolic meaning, may still be frightening. The machine may also have womb-like implications, or it may even be sexual.

Why is it disturbing to see patients lying on gurneys out in the corridors of hospitals, exposed and untended, as I saw occasionally on my visits? Perhaps because a hospital is a place of incubation, and a patient needs a cozy room that serves as a womb for incubating her illness.

The next time you pass a large hospital, think of all the people lying there in beds. From a purely physical viewpoint, they are resting and restoring their bodies. From the soul viewpoint, they are in a position of sleep and dream or even a kind of meditation. You could imagine them incubating their pasts and futures, making new sense of their lives.

Ancient Greeks suffering a serious illness would go to the temple of Asklepios, the god of healing, to spend a night on a bed and have a healing dream. The Greeks understood the mystery of healing, its connection to dream, and the importance of incubation. We still have the outward form, but we have forgotten the uses of dream.

The word *incubate* comes from the Latin *incubare*, "to lie on." To incubate is to "lie on" something to give it moderate heat so that it comes to life, like a bird sitting on an egg. Hospital patients are incubating their illnesses, lying in while full of fantasy. The illness takes away normal activities so that all the patient can do is reflect and simmer his thoughts and feelings.

In those hospital beds, emotions are also incubating. Just have a deep conversation with a patient and you will see how much fantasy has been wakened by illness. Sick people rarely tire of talking about what is wrong with them.

Some see this tendency as a kind of narcissism—they can't stop thinking about themselves. But it could be something deeper and more significant, like meditating in a focused way on everything that is wrong in their lives, not just their physical condition.

If the body is the soul, then when we are sick, not only our bodies but our souls, too, are sick, and the healing of the soul might heal the body as well. Medicine has yet to satisfactorily sort out the interplay of emotion and sickness. Today we talk about "stress," a generic term too broad to help us in specific diagnoses and treatments. One thing is clear: a doctor or nurse who can connect well with a patient helps the patient avoid sinking into depression or feeling isolated in his predicament.

When I saw Dr. Dinesh Kalra, my first cardiologist, he did not make a good impression. I had just come out of the treadmill room, where I had had a bad experience—the technicians got so involved in a heated discussion that they didn't see me nearly collapsing. The doctor was sitting at a screen, closely scrutinizing an ultrasound replay of my heart at work. He kept saying, "It's abnormal. It's abnormal"—that word again. He showed me the scan. "Look, the whole heart is not pumping. There is a portion in the back that is inactive. This is a problem. Something is wrong." He told me to visit him in his office in three days. The technicians told me to go home and do virtually nothing. I couldn't even walk or go to the store.

"Can't I play golf?" I asked them. I had just played nine holes the day before.

They looked at me as if I was crazy. "No walking at all," they said, and they looked worried and concerned. Naturally, I caught their anxiety like a head cold and lived with it for three days. You can imagine my nervous anticipation.

During the office visit, though, Dr. Kalra was more reassuring. "We can take care of it, whatever it is," he said.

In later visits he became much more relaxed, and soon I was grateful to have him as my cardiologist. He smiled at my anxieties and my tendency toward hypochondria. He told me that I was like his father, who always worried about pains here and there that meant nothing. He told me to walk three miles a day and relax more.

If I did indeed relax during this worrisome period when I had stents inserted into my heart, it was largely because of Dr. Kalra's attitude. He was competent but reassuring. My visits to him lasted only minutes, and yet he was fully present in those minutes as a positive, friendly human being as well as a skilled doctor. The combination, I'm sure, helped my healing.

Connection: A Sign of Soul

You can tell when doctors or nurses do their work with soul. They are present to you as people. They don't hide behind their professional masks or their routine chores. They give you their attention and relate to you, if only for a short time. Here we come upon another essential sign of soul—connection.

Soulful work is an activity in which you are engaged and involved. A soulful relationship goes deep and creates deep ties. A soulful family is one in which the members are involved in each other's lives and don't just live independently. The capacity to connect is a first step toward bringing soul to what you do and how you live.

Health-care professionals sometimes worry about being too involved with their patients, and so they go out of their way not to connect. Certainly some nurses and doctors work out their own emotional needs through their patients, perhaps by holding back disturbing information that could be useful or by offering excessive assurance. But the opposite problem seems to be more typical: keeping a distance for fear of being overly involved. The professional thinks that by being distant he or she will avoid pain at the death of a patient or a sense of loss on the day the patient goes home. He may also believe that a patient needs the assurance of a steeled professional who doesn't succumb to cheap emotion.

But there is a faulty psychology in this common belief in emotional disengagement. Disconnecting is a form of repression. You either have emotions or you don't. If you pretend you don't, even with the high purpose of maintaining your authority, you are suppressing feelings that will not go away without serious repercussions. Over time, a habit of concealing emotion makes for an emotionless, cool, distant personality. Further, following the psychoanalytic rule that the repressed always returns in worse form, those repressed emotions can erupt in many different problematic ways.

Some people repress their feelings and then, in spite of their habitual cool, easily fall in love, perhaps inappropriately. Or they may become chronically depressive or aggressive—sometimes the two emotions combine. The soulfulness has been hidden, but it reappears, as Jung often put it, with a terrible autonomy. You have little control over these resurfacing feelings and they may well come up in untimely and inappropriate settings. Medical television programs, like *House* and *Grey's Anatomy,* are built on this tendency in hospitals for relationships to become hysterical and emotions complicated beyond reason. Sexual acting-out also seems to go along with this.

A much better strategy is to trust your emotions. Yes, they can get out of hand, but less so when they are accepted as part of life and connected with your values and ideas. Repression is a kind of violence to the emotional life, cutting it off from other psychological resources. You can thoughtfully relate to people with an open heart but without being too open. You can connect to people in appropriate ways, being present, feeling a wide range of emotion, all the time knowing that your connection takes place within a limited arena, say the temporary relationship of patient and doctor.

The medical professional might benefit from a basic education in the psychology of human relationships. Patients are certainly going to "project" fantasies onto their doctors and nurses. They will see you as saviors, magicians, confessors, geniuses, and even lovers. If you're aware, you can spot those projections and deal with them compassionately and clearly.

Psychotherapists understand these projections as a form of transference, shifting past established patterns onto present circumstances and people. Doctors and nurses are equal targets for transference. Here are some simple rules for dealing with patients' projections:

- Expect exaggerated fantasies about you and your role.

- Respond to these excessive expectations in a realistic and measured manner.

- Don't get caught in the fantasies by playing the role of the genius, the magician, or the lover. Make an effort to reveal yourself for exactly who you are.

- Don't simply avoid patients who have an erroneous impression of you or try to detonate the fantasies by interpreting them away. Some doctors distance themselves from people who adore them or expect too much from them, whereas they could instead stay close and let the illusions go past them and probably evaporate.

- Talk to trusted friends and colleagues about them. Compare notes.

- Read some basic articles or books about transference and emotion. Educate yourself psychologically.

By being an emotional person who knows how to set limits without repressing feelings, you will have the ability to connect to your patients and in that way contribute to their healing, and still be free to enjoy some distance without becoming cold.

The Soulful Professional

Another sign of soul is the capacity to love: to love your work, love your patients, love your workplace, and love your calling. This is asking for a lot. But love need not be gushing and all-absorbing. It may be a steady appreciation and the joy of doing what you want to do and what best fulfills you.

Modern medicine offers many obstacles to this kind of love. The long hours, the extensive education, the threat of lawsuits, the pressures of insurance, the machinations of hospitals and groups—all of these factors, and more, make the life of a doctor or nurse difficult and sometimes impossible. In November 2008, The Physicians' Foundation released the results of a survey of over 300,000 doctors, noting that 49 percent said that over the next three years they plan to reduce the number of patients they see or stop practicing entirely.[3]

In my own interviews with health-care workers I found that the great majority loved their work and their patients. Generally they had mixed feelings about the organizations they worked for, and virtually all had complaints about

Medicare and insurance. Doctors and nurses tend to enjoy working with patients and doing research and despise all the paperwork they have to attend to regularly.

In connection with love and the soul, one interesting comment we heard from nurses in various specialties had to do with the psychological aspects of their work. Physical-rehab nurses and those working in the oncology areas told us that they felt that 90 percent of their work was psychological. Helping people deal emotionally with new limitations in life and the threat of dying was a major part of their job, though it wasn't in their job description and they were not educated for it.

Where these nurses used the word *psychological*, I might refer to the soul. Their patients needed to find a new source of meaning and a calming of their anxieties in the face of serious accident or illness. Nurses spoke of just sitting at patients' bedsides or checking in on them before quitting time as being an important part of their job.

Modern medicine impresses with its polysyllabic and Latinized language, its arcane information, and its sophisticated machinery. The soul is not as impressive. Its concerns and methods are so ordinary and usually so simple that they are easily dismissed as irrelevant and unworthy. What is so astonishing about a chaplain being aware of the suffering of a psychotic patient? What is so remarkable about a hospice worker baking banana bread for a dying patient? Why worry about the colors and textures of a hospital room? Compare these concerns with brain surgery.

A soulful medical professional is comfortable with his or her humanity, plain and simple. He doesn't have to be above common emotions or above making mistakes. He can talk to patients as people and can be around them as a human being, not only as an expert.

This is one of the key ideas of a book written in the 16th century at the home of Thomas More of England, the humanist and lawyer executed by Henry VIII for not approving the royal divorce and a secular leader as head of the Church. One of More's longtime friends, Erasmus of Rotterdam, once visited More at his home in England for an extended stay. During his visit he wrote what is perhaps his most famous book, *Encomium Moriae* (In Praise of Foolishness). The title is a pun on the name of his host— *moria* in Greek means "fool." Among other things, the book observes that human beings connect to each other best in their foolishness. Erasmus blasts the experts and intellectuals, giving an important lesson that applies in medicine— hiding behind your expertise will only distance you further from your colleagues and your patients.

One of the consistent teachings in many spiritual traditions concerns the importance of knowing your limits and being fully aware of what you don't know. According to the "bible" of Chinese Taoism, the Tao Te Ching, "The Tao that can be known is not the eternal Tao." One of the most brilliant of Renaissance Christian theologians, Nicolas of Cusa, called his most famous book *De Docta Ignorantia* (Cultivated Ignorance). In it, he refers to *sacra ignorantia* or sacred ignorance.

"Even to the person devoted to learning nothing more wonderful could happen than to be conscious of the very ignorance that is special to him. He will be more intelligent to the extent that he is aware of his own ignorance."[4] Imagine a doctor who would follow this advice. He would be connected to humanity and probably comfortable with his patients, and they with him. But it is difficult in the modern medical environment to let on that you don't know something. You are supposed to be highly skilled, miraculously competent, and confident beyond all measure.

The trick is to be competent, confident, and comfortable with human limitation. Or perhaps a better way to put it: to be intelligent and skillful in technical aspects of medicine and equally wise and practiced in dealing with people. The idea that it is sufficient to be technically skillful betrays a materialistic and highly limited idea of what a person—a patient—is.

For 12 years now I have been giving a one-week summer course on Cape Cod sponsored by the New England Educational Institute. The first few years were particularly difficult. Many physicians participated in the class and objected to my "soft" humanities approach. They expected research results and carefully tabulated demographics. I was giving them mythology and poetry.

A few doctors, however, have been comfortable enough with their ignorance to open their minds to a humanities approach to medicine. They have discovered that not knowing everything can be a blessing, leaving room for new and deepening discoveries.

Cultivating the precious gifts of ignorance, you not only open your mind to new life, you also find what you have in common with the rest of humanity. The doctor who thinks he knows everything will never enjoy common ground with his patients. But once he or she learns that he can have a better relationship with his patients when he gives up the need for omniscience, he will be relaxed enough to connect with people at that low place of human imperfection and limitation.

Dr. Bettina Peyton has been a close friend, medical advisor, and inspiration for me for many years. She is on the board of directors of a hospice in Nashua, New Hampshire, where she cares for patients and teaches health-care workers the spirit and soul of care for dying patients. I told her that I was writing about the difficulty doctors have with the limits of their knowledge.

"Oh, yes," she said. "It's very difficult for a doctor to admit that he doesn't know something and to work constantly under the pressure to be all-knowing. But every day I have to say 'I don't know the answer.'"

"What do you mean?" I asked. "What sorts of questions can't you answer?"

"Will my family be all right? What happens after death? Will I continue on in some way? I think there is a form of survival after death, but I can't tell my patients that as a professional."

Dr. Peyton's questions, of course, are the ultimate ones, the mysteries that have no fixed and universal answers. It would be good if doctors asked themselves these impossible questions and reflected on them. They might then be ready to talk to patients who are facing their mortality and dealing with the ultimate leave-taking. Psychologists and spiritual counselors are an important resource, but doctors and nurses have an ongoing relationship with their patients, and their ability to discuss the difficult questions, if only briefly, may well be part of the overall healing of the patient.

The Body Expresses the Soul

"Diseases of the soul are more dangerous and more numerous than those of the body," said Cicero. The human soul goes through many powerful experiences over a lifetime, experiences that get etched on the face and in the body's posture and habits. I know a man who always jabs his finger at you when he's talking. You wonder where he picked up that habit and what particular feeling or point of view it expresses. You see people with faces of ease or fear or suffering and bodies gradually sculpted to express the kind of lives they have led. It isn't much of a step further to understand how the soul shows its struggles and achievements in illness and health.

The soul has more diseases than the body does because the soul has other avenues of expression. It can reveal its struggle in speech, behavior, attitude, and ways of relating. But its intimacy with the body comes through most clearly when the body suffers. Recently a woman in England told me of her lifelong struggle to speak her truth, be herself, and show her power. She held her hand on her belly when she said this. She knew that in Indian spiritual maps of the body, personal power resides in the area of the upper abdomen. But then she said that her words and wishes get stuck in her throat. She can get them to rise that far, but then she keeps them to herself. "Do you get sore throats?" I asked.

"All the time," she said.

A yogi would examine this situation in terms of the chakras, seven key points on the body where certain life issues find a focus. A third-chakra (abdomen) issue of power becomes a physical problem in a higher chakra, the throat. Some people, of course, keep it in the belly and get colitis and other abdominal maladies. Marsilio Ficino, a Renaissance philosopher and magus, once said that Mars, the spirit of power and aggression, can dissolve the intestines. When I first read that sentence, I was reminded of several acquaintances who had been treated for colitis and colon cancer and, sure enough, had trouble manifesting their individuality and their own thoughts and feelings.

Susan Sontag warns us against blaming people for their illnesses, but to inquire into the role of the soul in an illness, with an eye toward treating it holistically, is not the same as blame. At least, it shouldn't be. Perhaps one has to be careful, in looking for maladies of soul in physical complaints, not to slip into blaming the patient.

Psyche/Soma

One might expect psychosomatic medicine to present a solution to the problem of body and soul. After all, *psycho-somatic* means "soul-body"—*psyche,* soul; *soma,* body. But psychosomatic medicine has not yet fulfilled its promise. We have a long way to go before we incorporate close attention to a patient's relationships and life situation in an examination of his health.

One big problem with psychosomatic medicine is its being lodged in the purely scientific approach to medicine. Currently it is largely research- and evidence-based and subjected to all the anxious protocols of modernist practice. Although psyche means soul, you rarely come across a reference to soul in psychosomatic literature. Currently we suffer a split between scientism, an excessive belief in rationalistic methods, and a New Age appeal to spiritualism. One side is suspicious of the other, and the notion of soul is surrendered to the approaches that don't get respect from the scientific side.

But it would be useful, in fact it is crucial, that medicine consider persons as made up of body, soul, and spirit, reuniting psyche and soma in a less abstract and mechanistic manner. I notice that members of psychosomatic societies are almost all M.D.'s, while professionals in religious studies, depth psychology, anthropology, and even the arts would add immeasurably to our understanding of the spirit and soul in illness.

Psychosomatic medicine has a long and significant future, but only if it broadens its concerns beyond limited scientific studies and approaches the phenomenology of emotion, meaning, personal history, and the images in illness. Only a comprehensive and somewhat intuitive investigation of illness will reveal connections between meaning, emotion, and disease.

CHAPTER 3

THE HEALING MILIEU

Many people expect talk of the soul to be abstract and ethereal, but tradition speaks of the soul as the mediator or link between body and spirit. It has certain spiritual inclinations, but it is also closely related to physical life. The Chinese say that the body is the physical life of the soul—an elegant way of putting it. Generally, the soul has to do with the intimate and ordinary details of daily life.

In considering the soul of medicine, a major concern is the physical place in which healing occurs. If it is soulful, then the practice of medicine will have a much better chance of having soul as well. For that reason, the design and furnishing of a hospital, clinic, or doctor's office, or, more specifically, a patient's room, an operating room, or a reception and entrance area, is critical.

The architecture of a modern doctor's office often conveys subliminal messages that have deep roots—both in the sense of primal feelings and historical antecedents. The first thing you see may be a glass barrier between the waiting room and the mysterious, labyrinthine hallways and examining rooms behind the barrier. In those rooms you subject yourself to probes, needles, nakedness, and the threat of bad news. The ancient healing sites of the medicine god Asklepios, in Greece, included a round building, called the *tholos,* with an underground maze of passages that some think housed the snakes that were associated with Asklepios.

Does the doctor's office echo this tholos? Is there something deep and archetypal about the medical labyrinth? If so, it may be useful to bring out the symbolic and ritual aspects of the labyrinth, instead of presenting it as merely functional. In most things today, given our modernist tendencies, the rich and important symbolic aspects of our life and work go underground and are lived unconsciously. In that way they appear confusing and fail to address the significant needs of the soul.

Imagine if your journey from the receptionist's station to the examining room involved an initiatory walk through hallways carefully designed and decorated and fitted with statues of the healing Buddha and the like? What if your walk to the small cubicle led you into the sanctuary of healing through deep feeling and imagination?

In order to create such a labyrinth, we would need to have reached a point culturally where we understand the spiritual dimension of every illness and all treatment. We could do this while preserving our valuable secularity, and what I'm talking about has nothing to do with belief in God. It is merely appreciating the spiritual aspect of medicine and illness as a soul initiation.

A contemporary observer would insist that the maze of hallways today is purely functional, that there is no reference to archaic rituals. But nothing comes into being without the human imagination. You can't build what you can't imagine. And the imagination doesn't always remain in a limited time frame. Ancient ideas creep undetected into modern ways of doing things. I would argue that they are archetypal, so deep in the psyche that they have a long history and emerge without much thought.

Joseph Campbell often talked about the mythic hero having to cross a dangerous threshold before he could get on with the discovery of new life. The way between the known and familiar realm, on one side, and the unfamiliar and renewing on the other was guarded by an ogre, a frightening being who usually had to be outwitted before the hero could make any progress.

Campbell's description could apply to receptionists and guides who are posted at the entries of hospitals and doctors' offices: "It is only by advancing beyond those bounds, provoking the destructive aspect of the same power [that heals], that the individual passes into a new zone of experience."[5] In another place, Campbell refers to statues of beasts that often stand guard at the entrance to a cemetery. These are the threshold guardians that we still encounter in medicine as receptionists. Notice your feelings when you are asked to present your insurance card and personal information. You may well feel that you are being challenged and vetted by the guardian at the gate.

Once approved and admitted, and having traversed the labyrinth, you sit in a small examining room, waiting for the doctor to arrive, with little to meditate on but chrome instruments, tongue depressors, and plastic models of body organs of unnatural color. You might detect the pungent aroma of some chemical you wouldn't want in your body. Here, aromatherapy has something positive to offer. Imagine carefully designed good smells surrounding you as you prepare for diagnosis and treatment.

In the examining cubicle you can do nothing but think, and the place, designed for function rather than a spirituality of health, bends your thoughts toward pain, discomfort, and bad news. Knowing that people are usually alone with their thoughts for an extended time in these tiny rooms, architects and decorators could make them in such a way that the patient is calmed, comforted, and even inspired during those captive moments of reflection.

Entering a hospital or medical center is often a nightmare. Obsessed with worry about your health, you go through doors that separate you from the world you love and enter a realm where you will be a stranger and at the mercy of nurses and orderlies. First, you have to deal with money, signing insurance forms and giving your credit card, which offers its own level of anxiety. You have to fill out questionnaires and have a plastic band secured to your wrist. Are you a patient or an inmate? Is this a hospital (meaning a place of hospitality) or a prison?

Religious specialists, like me, are particularly interested in what we call liminality—the experience of any kind of threshold. Most churches effectively lead you from the secular world outside to the spiritual realm inside through large, thick, ornate doors and a transitional vestibule or entry that allows you to take the initiatory step of encountering sacred space. A door is not just a physical barrier; it is also an instrument of psychological passage. A purely functional door will get you into the hospital physically, but it takes a special doorway to get your soul in.

Some medical buildings employ a large, expensive atrium for liminality, but a potent architectural detail—an impressive door, flowing water, a grotto, hushed lighting, or a massive stone—could also do the job. These are all traditional ritual objects that are effective for transitions.

One day I toured a large hospital with the man in charge of the "hospital environment." I asked him to take me first to the entrance that most people would use. It was a series of glass doors leading from a parking structure to a broad hallway flanked by two other, narrower corridors in the form of a T. There was no art and no special architecture, only the plain glass doors, through which, from inside the hospital, you had a view of the parked cars. My guide had no idea why I was dismayed.

"It's great," he said. "People can go right from their cars into the main corridor, where signs tell them exactly where everything is."

"Useful," I thought, "but can a patient make the transition from world to healing space by means of those doors?" There is nothing wrong with functionality. Functional design can be beautiful, though sometimes it is ugly simply because there is no other thought given to the design beyond function. An exclusive emphasis on function leaves nothing for the soul. Patients in this hospital enter with their modern Cartesian bodies and leave their souls in the car.

What is the patient's or family's *experience* of entering this building? First, they glimpse the interior, with all its commotion and confusion, before they go through the doors. They find themselves in a liminal space, all right, between a parking garage and a manic hospital corridor. This liminal space inspires confusion and anxiety. No wonder there is staff posted there to direct patients and families entering.

Next, the unwary visitors are immediately faced with a decision whether to go straight or turn left or right. "There are signs everywhere," the man assured me. Yes, signs. You have to use your head, not your intuition or your bodily sense of place, in order to proceed. Signs inform but do not initiate. They speak to the mind but don't appeal to the whole person. And they clutter the entryway, like billboards at the approach to a town.

Because the signs are substitutes for a deep, guiding architecture, they appear as clutter. They stand in the way of anything beautiful about the entrance, and beauty is essential for the soul. If any part of a hospital should be designed and built beautifully, it is the entrance. How you enter affects everything else that takes place.

At the hospital in question, should the signs fail, a patient could approach a small information desk to the side of the main hallway. Here again the hospital offers information but not passage. The feng shui is not good, because the guardian sits at a tiny, insignificant desk off to the side.

The information desk could be much more impressive, perhaps large and more ornate, certainly more beautiful. Approaching it should be an experience that gives you pause and affects you emotionally. If the information desk is pedestrian and the guardian merely functional, the role of guardian will go underground and become negative. Not only will the patient lack a means of deep entry into a healing space, the guardian might be difficult to deal with. Whenever you have a modern functional replacement for an archaic ritual figure, you not only lose the power of ritual, you encounter a person who doesn't know what his job really is. He is confused and so are the patients.

Here, then, is another rule about the soul: It is affected by symbol, ritual, and image. None of this has to be understood or registered intellectually; it is enough to experience the transition of a good entry or the spirit of healing in a well-designed examining and treatment area. Of course, it takes an architect and artist educated in traditional ritual space to design an effective entry. A soulful healing environment will reflect sensitivity to the symbolic import of everything in sight: materials, sounds, smells, images, language, and uniforms.

Natural Materials

Illness arrives like an unwanted guest, usually as a dark, creeping surprise. It seems to come from nowhere and appears in the body as from underground. In religion, underground spirits are called *chthonic*, meaning "of the earth." A cave, an underground spring, a grave, and a crypt are all chthonic. Many illnesses have this chthonic aspect. They go unnoticed until one day they appear in a rash, a fever, or a lump. A lump is a fascinating chthonic medical phenomenon. I would love to read a good phenomenological/psychological study of the experience of lumps.

It makes sense, then, to use artistic, ritual, and architectural chthonic images in hospitals and clinics. A spring, a fountain, a pit, a well, or an alcove may suggest the hidden aspect of an illness, so that the architecture participates in the experience and is congruent with both illness and healing.

I have visited one school and one hospice where, in each case, the architect designed a stream to flow inside the building. As you walk through the halls, occasionally you pass over this stream and are aware of a level of life just beneath ordinary activity. Your attention is drawn downward to a level usually ignored. Religious tradition suggests that this is the realm of the gods and nature spirits, and therefore it is important to acknowledge this area in medicine.

Streams and fountains have the added value of representing the flow of life, an image often associated with healing. In Ireland I have visited many holy wells that are usually hidden out in fields and on hills, surrounded by protective trees, where people of the area even today come daily for the healing water. We could create healing wells in our hospitals, or at least install fountains and ponds that hint at the holy, healing well. Any moving water, whether a stream or a wall of flowing water, also evokes the spirit of healing. The Greeks referred to the atmosphere created by pools, streams, and marshes as nymphs. A good artist and architect could evoke one of these healing nymphs and transform a functional health-care operation into a place of healing.

In one of the simplest and yet most profound sayings ever recorded, the Greek mystic Herakleitos said, "Everything flows." This is the secret of all secrets. Life flows, time keeps moving, nothing stands still. This is the way of life and a sign of health. You try to stop life, freeze it, and keep it from moving on, and you get sick. Flowing water is therefore the basic image for health and one that every healing environment should incorporate in art or ritual form. A stream or waterfall would evoke the mystery best, but short of that, a small version—a pumped model waterfall or pond, even desk-size, or a photograph or painting—would do.

Besides water, other natural materials in the architecture and furnishings of a hospital, clinic, or home sickroom help evoke the healing powers of nature and the body. Natural wood, plants and flowers, growing grains, animals, iron, natural fabrics, stone, and clay and ceramic are also evocative.

Another spirit that would enliven the soul is nature as mother, the one the Greeks called Demeter and the Romans Ceres, from whom we get our word *cereal*. Many makers of supplements and vitamins appear to be inspired by this particular spirituality. You find this Mother Nature in the names of companies—Nature's Bounty, All Natural, Nature's Way, Food Origins. Many medical centers these days are creating rooftop and cloister gardens in formerly empty spaces. They could include grasses and grains to evoke Demeter as a spirit of health.

It is best to have actual objects of nature, even if they are miniature, like a small Zen garden or a bonsai tree or even a desk waterfall or fountain. Better to make furnishings out of natural materials and build a "green" structure from scratch. But you might also place paintings and photographs of nature throughout the healing environment. Children love to draw nature, so they could help fit out a children's area.

I've seen patients' art in some hospitals, and these efforts can be moving. My wife, Hari Kirin, a skilled and profound painter herself, often teaches people how to make real art even if they don't consider themselves artists. Both naïve and professional art have a place in the making of the healing milieu, but professional art has special powers of beauty and inspiration.

Everyone benefits when you contract artists for paintings, sculptures, gardens, photographs, ceramics, architectural detail, furnishings, and soundscapes. An artist has the calling, the skills, the imagination, and the experience to skillfully create images that have power. We wouldn't think of inviting an amateur to remove a kidney, but we don't distinguish well between amateur and professional art. A well-designed visual and aural setting for healing activity is of great importance in supporting the work of medical experts. Besides, every community has its artists in need of financial support, community recognition, and an audience.

Images and the Therapeutic Milieu

Waiting for the doctor is a simple act but full of fantasy and emotion. You sit in a waiting room with other patients, wondering what is wrong with them. You are in a community of the infirm, almost like a level beneath normal life but not quite in the underworld—a chthonic community. You're provided with magazines to distract you from the Underworld journey that you're on.

Not long before he died of ALS, or Lou Gehrig's disease, I worked a few times with Phil Simmons, a highly intelligent, gifted writer and teacher. Once, he and I were giving a talk for the McGill University Faculty of Medicine when someone asked him, based on his experience as a patient, what he would most like to see changed in modern medicine. "I'd like to see them update the magazines in waiting areas," he said with his usual smile.

Maybe the dated, well-fingered magazines are meant to distract from the dark business at hand, but they evoke death and decay. The news is no longer fresh and the photographs appear to be from another era. It doesn't take long for magazines to age.

I usually use waiting time for a certain kind of meditating. I don't accept the magazines that are offered and I try to get as far from the ever-present television as possible. I have nothing against television and enjoy certain programs at home, but not while waiting to be treated medically. This is a time for serious consideration. The magazines and loud televisions are supposed to remove you from your experience, but I prefer a room without distractions. So I sit calmly in a Zen spirit, taking everything in. I don't close my eyes and I don't sit in any particular posture. I just sit.

Modern culture has yet to discover the healing powers of quiet, to say nothing of silence. Medical buildings are usually deep into the modern spirit in this regard. No one seems to notice the noise of the television set anchored to the ceiling as if destined to broadcast for eternity.

The Healing Sound of Quiet

A healing milieu is a quiet one. While it's true that the sound of life and vitality can cheer up a patient who is sad about his illness, excessive noise can make a hospital or medical center a place of torture rather than healing. Studies tell what we know intuitively, that a quiet environment lowers blood pressure and promotes healing.

But noise and quiet often don't enter the awareness of a busy health-care worker. The sounds of machines, chatter, slamming doors and cabinets, and public announcements and pages are enough to disturb the rest of patients in serious need of calm. They create an atmosphere of excessive activity and frenzy. In the course of my research, many times I met with nurses on their units in messy, busy rooms on floors littered with machinery, computers, and storage cabinets. These created both aural and visual noise.

Not only patients but workers too benefit from a lowering of decibels. There is enough anxiety about performance on a hospital floor or in a doctor's office. There is no need to intensify that anxiety with noise.

In an aptly titled essay, "The Inhospitable Hospital," nurse Laura Stokowski writes about the health impact of quiet and highlights neonatal care in a hospital, an area where loud sounds are common and yet particularly dangerous for the patients.[6] Stokowski has a few suggestions for decreasing the noise level that apply in all medical environments:

- Lower telephone volume
- Change to ring binders that close quietly
- Dampen cabinet doors and drawers
- Educate housekeeping staff about noise
- Use "Quiet, Please" posters

These suggestions are useful. They are practical and detailed. But what we need more than anything else is an overall appreciation for quiet and the personal discovery of how beneficial quiet can be.

Learning how to be quiet and understand its value to health could be part of a health-care worker's education and training—a course in silence. We can't assume that people know such things naturally or through their own education. I had an unusual education, as I spent my youth in a religious order living a quasi-monastic lifestyle. For example, we observed "the great silence" from 9:00 P.M. to 9:00 A.M. That included meditation from 5:15 A.M. to 6:00 A.M., Mass, chant, breakfast in silence, a silent walk outdoors, spiritual reading for 15 minutes, and then, when the silence ended, classes. One day each month and one week every year we went on a silent retreat. As a musician I developed a sensitive ear, and as a monk I learned the beauty of silence.

Quiet isn't just the absence of noise and sound. Quiet can include sounds that create calm and can also come from architecture and décor that is quiet. A careful selection of music and calming sounds of nature can contribute to a healing milieu. Water fountains and streams, wind, and birds can help create a peaceful atmosphere that is still lively and positive. Color and shape can also be either noisy or calm. Alcoves, fireplaces, and well-designed and well-placed objects like vases and flowers and soft chairs; muted but warm colors; and fabrics and textiles and natural materials can all help make an active place quiet.

A quiet environment is not a passive one. In a quiet space you can hear your thoughts and feel your emotions. That's why noise is often a defense against experiencing your life. Many people don't want to know what they are experiencing.

Planetree

On a classically crisp fall day in 2008, I visited Griffin Hospital in Derby, Connecticut, which happens to be the headquarters of an organization devoted to patient-centered health care called Planetree. I went with two friends, Rev. Mark McKinney and Sharon O'Brien, who were my colleagues at Saint Francis in Hartford. Sometime in the 1990s I met Mark, who had created a unique position in pastoral care at Saint Francis. He took a course with me on Cape Cod one summer, where I met his family. He had educated himself in a broad approach to spirituality and had mastered the archetypal psychology that James Hillman and a few close friends had created in the 1970s and 1980s.

Mark arranged for me to give a few lectures over several years at Saint Francis, and in 2007 I proposed to him that I visit the hospital regularly. I could get valuable information and context for my writing on medicine, and I would do what I could to bring ideas of soul and spirit to Saint Francis. The arrangement worked out better than I could have hoped for, and Mark and I, joined by Sharon O'Brien, manager of the integrative-medicine department of the hospital, met once a month with staff from every department.

On that fall day in Connecticut we were all impressed with the Planetree hospital. Approaching the building a block away, we found it nondescript and boxy, but once we parked in the hospital lot we began to see innovation.

We got out of the car and heard music, good music, from speakers in the parking lot. The entrance was not dramatic or symbolic, but I was impressed to note that the first thing that met you inside the hospital was a very active patient/staff library. Information and education here were a top priority. Then we noticed carpeting throughout the hospital, and graceful furniture—many well-furnished gathering points for families, complete with small tables and chairs for children. Almost every corner of every room had a beautiful vase on a table or just sitting on a counter. The nurses' stations had no floor-to-ceiling barriers but were quiet and inviting. Patients' rooms looked like bedrooms. The dining room had a handsome fireplace and served healthy food. Even the few vending machines offered organic snacks.

A glance at Planetree's mission statement tells us that it's possible in these action-oriented times to pay attention to the human side of things:

We Believe . . .

- that we are human beings, caring for other human beings

- we are all caregivers

- caregiving is best achieved through kindness and compassion

- safe, accessible, high-quality care is fundamental to patient-centered care

- in a holistic approach to meeting people's needs of body, mind, and spirit

- families, friends, and loved ones are vital to the healing process

- access to understandable health information can empower individuals to participate in their health care

- the opportunity for individuals to make personal choices related to their care is essential

- physical environments can enhance healing, health, and well-being

- illness can be a transformational experience for patients, families, and caregivers

Susan Frampton, the sophisticated and energetic president of Planetree, assured me that her organization is always trying to push the edge of its patient-centered philosophy, exploring new ideas and possibilities. I was certainly impressed with all it had accomplished, including a waterfall just outside its new oncology center.

This Planetree hospital confirmed my idea that special attention to patients as persons and to their families, supported by a peaceful and graceful physical environment, could transform health care. It also demonstrated how the staff in such a medical setting benefits as well. They work in quiet, comfortable, rather private settings, as evocative of home as are the rooms of the patients. You can see signs of their teamwork in the architecture of the place.

When people first hear about Planetree, they question the cost of this kind of care and wonder if it is only for the elite. But Dr. Frampton pointed out several examples of thoughtful choices made for beauty and quiet that had no additional cost. All that was required was concern for values beyond practicality and efficiency and a steady commitment to the vision of whole patient health care.

Living the Vision

One interesting lesson to be taken from Planetree is the combination of vision and detail. You have to keep the overall principles in mind as a guiding structure, but you have to implement that vision in every small detail, from furnishing to doctor-patient interaction. You have to think constantly of patient-centered medicine, and then you have to keep in mind every minute of every day what a whole person is so that you address your patients as persons.

This matter of maintaining your vision brings up a question that slowly took form for me as I visited one hospital and medical center after another. Do you hope that you will get people on your staff who have the vision and personality needed to create good relations and a healing milieu, or do you create a community of care and train a staff to treat patients as persons?

I presented this question to Sister Judy Carey at Saint Francis Hospital in Hartford. Sister Judy is vice president of mission integration at Saint Francis. One evening, following a lecture at the hospital, I spoke with Sister Judy about her work. Huddled in the crowd, she told me about the mission statement of the hospital and how she took it very seriously and wanted to make sure that every staff member knew it and lived by it every day.

It was Sister Judy who taught me how to go beyond hoping for gifted personnel and instead inspire and train people to act caringly and humanely in their daily activities.

She also told me that being true to the mission statement was a major factor in hiring and keeping staff members.

The mission statement reflects the Catholic heritage of the hospital:

Our Mission
We are committed to health and healing through excellence, compassionate care, and reverence for the spirituality of each person.

Our Core Values
Respect. We honor the worth and dignity of those we serve and with whom we work.
Integrity. We are faithful, trustworthy, and just.
Service. We reach out to the community, especially those most in need.
Leadership. We encourage initiative, creativity, learning, and research.
Stewardship. We care for and strengthen resources entrusted to us.

Long after I had gotten to know Sister Judy fairly well, we sat down and talked again about the mission. This time she emphasized the word *reverence,* and I was reminded of Albert Schweitzer's philosophy of work: reverence for life.

It helps greatly to have a philosophy of life that is an elaboration of a spiritual vision and set of standards for making decisions and responding to people. Without a philosophy of life you have to improvise constantly. With a philosophy, a mission statement if you will, you don't have to think through every decision from the ground up. You have a vision that guides you. It's best if you can summarize that vision in a few words.

Once, when I mentioned this idea to an audience in Keene, New Hampshire, someone asked me what my philosophy was. I knew, but I hadn't reduced it to a few words. Now I might say, "Foster individual creativity."

Personal freedom means everything to me. I see many well-intentioned people regularly telling others how to think, which words to use, and exactly how to do things, and making judgments afterwards. A mild fascism characterizes the social interactions of many people. My own philosophy moves in the opposite direction. As a teacher, I like to inspire students to think on their own and make their own decisions, learning from their mistakes as well as their achievements. In my books I don't tell people how to live; I raise issues and explore them, hoping that the discussion will educate the reader in his or her own way.

With regard to patients undergoing medical treatment, I apply my philosophy by asking doctors and nurses to respect the individuality of their patients. Don't boss them around. Trust their ideas. Don't worry when they go against protocol. With regard to colleagues and staff, respect their ideas and support their initiatives.

The most common complaint I heard from nurses was doctors' habit of disregarding their ideas and expertise. Hospitals run in part on doctors' fascism, the need many of them have to be in complete control. Many doctors have a similar attitude toward patients—they should do exactly what the expert tells them. It's dangerous for them to think for themselves.

The image of the doctor as medical despot is crumbling, but not without complaint. Patients are educating themselves about their illnesses and asking specific questions. They are moving out beyond the perimeters of Western medicine. They are taking responsibility for their health. This should be a good change for doctors. Now they can guide an educated public rather than take more responsibility than is required.

Back to Sister Judy, her idea of respect and reverence applies to the way staff members talk to each other and to their patients. If they are not kind and respectful, and Sister Judy hears about it, she will have a word with those people and remind them of the mission. She herself wears the mission statement on a pin at all times, and she takes every opportunity to express it and encourage its values.

This is an answer to my question. How do you get staff to treat people well at all times? You remind them constantly of the core values and you teach and sanction these values. You make a project out of implementing a common philosophy. You live it in every situation and model it in the most ordinary settings.

It isn't a coincidence that Sister Judy is a Catholic sister or that Saint Francis was founded by sisters who came from France. A philosophy of service is a spiritual achievement. As we move into the 21st century, one major change we can make is to bring spiritual values into secular enterprises. This is far different from forcing particular values on a secular society. It is a nondenominational spirituality, in which many faiths and even agnostic philosophies can contribute. It is a spirituality completely compatible with the precious secularity of our institutions of health.

CHAPTER 4

THE
SPIRITUALITY
OF MEDICINE

The connection between spirituality and healing is widespread and deep among the many traditions. Jesus is a healer, as are shamans, spiritual teachers, and the Buddha. Previously I've mentioned the religious iconography that shows the Lapis Lazuli Radiant Healing Buddha as a colorful, peaceful, and comforting healing presence. In this form the Buddha is shown surrounded by a brilliant blue color as he holds a bowl of medicines in one hand and a healing plant in the other.

Vows associated with this Buddha urge the caregiver to heal with his presence and his radiance. We see this radiance in the halo around Jesus's head and the radiant background to various depictions of the Buddha. But we all have halos and auras. We all radiate the quality of our souls, both good and bad. It doesn't take much to pick up the radiance of care around a nurse or the radiance of expertise behind a doctor.

In a day's time most people go through a wide range of emotions and are not consistently radiant. But there can be no doubt that a generally positive, caring radiance in the presence of a doctor or nurse is better for a patient than a neurotic one. Big-ego radiance is not reassuring, nor is repressed-anger aura.

There is nothing surreal or supernatural about this kind of radiance. It may come from having a strong vision in relation to your calling, joined by dedication and experience. Feeling called to the work marks the beginning of a spiritual dimension. You are not just doing a job, and you're not just a technician. Your whole being is involved in your work. People see it in the air around you.

About five years after *Care of the Soul* came out, I received a manuscript from a doctor who was working with AIDS patients in a New York hospital. Dr. Daniel Baxter's perceptive approach to his patients and the stories he told about them inspired me. Here was a doctor who could draw on genuine spiritual resources without all the baggage of excessive piety and anxieties about belief. He understood that the spiritual component is part of what a person is, and in gritty ways he struggled with his difficult patients to unleash their own kind of spirituality.

"There appears to be something in the dying human mind that tries to put to rest any conflicts, to make sense of a lifetime of experiences," he explained. "As Tolstoy wrote of Ivan Ilych, it is never too late for a person to find the 'real thing' in his or her life."[7]

Putting conflicts to rest and making sense of a life are two important spiritual tasks for a dying patient. Dr. Baxter sees it as part of his job description to participate in these activities during a person's last days. Further, he understands that the tasks his patients try to avoid and deny and put off are those that he himself will one day have to face. He doesn't divide himself in his role of expert from his own humanity.

One sometimes hears spirituality discussed as though it were an external sheet of graceful language and ritual that you place like a veil over a person in extreme circumstances. In fact, the spiritual issues are the most difficult of all—finding meaning when the universe has let you down, finding love when your friends and family feel rejected, and finding peace when every bit of news torments and depresses you.

Spirituality always involves some kind of transcending of limitations and challenges. You find more strength than you knew you had. You don't succumb to resignation and cynicism. You go beyond your narcissism or your worry about yourself. You arrive at peace with your fate. These are all spiritual achievements, even if they lack the usual language of the churches and traditions.

For Chaplains It's a New World

In my research for this book I talked to a wide variety of chaplains and pastoral counselors. My impression is that the opportunities for chaplains to offer realistic and useful spiritual guidance to people have never been greater, but neither have the obstacles been more challenging.

Today people seem divided more than ever along liberal/conservative lines. There isn't much middle ground between old-fashioned literal belief and the newer emphasis on personal spiritual care and development. In general, older people are attached to their church, their clergy, and their beliefs, while younger people are looking for spiritual care where they can find it. This is a generalization, of course, because you can find open-minded older people and extremely conservative young ones.

A similar division characterizes chaplains, who may be old-fashioned in their theology or free-thinking when it comes to tradition. I heard several stories of chaplains entering patient's rooms and immediately offering to pray with them or bless them or give them a sacrament (if Catholic). Faced with a rushed, pushy chaplain, a patient might ask him or her to leave or simply not be open to what the chaplain can offer. As one professor of pastoral counseling told me, "These guys have to learn to listen first and talk later. They barge into a patient's room and expect to be treated like royalty. They have to earn a patient's respect first by listening and learning who the patient is."

A chaplain's theology and attitude about spiritual guidance translates into a style that will be either authoritative or responsive. More people today have complex feelings and ideas about the spiritual life than perhaps people in the past had. They don't want to be told what to do or what they should believe. They want guidance, not direction.

A good pastoral counselor or chaplain can listen to a patient and find out quickly what he needs and what style of approach is appropriate to him. A traditional chaplain can ease up on the authority and instead offer spiritual guidance. Even in the old theology, the one in which I was brought up, spiritual counseling was a subset of religious practice. Spirituality and religion were wedded to each other, not separated as they are now.

A more liberal-minded chaplain can give conservative patients the prayers and comfort they want and in small ways tend to their personal spiritual issues. A chaplain doesn't have to be as polarized as the people she serves. She can be more sophisticated, more flexible, and more open to individual needs.

When my mother was dying, a priest came to her bedside. She was an extremely devout Catholic; her religion meant everything to her, and though a bit open-minded, she really only understood the religion of her childhood. The elderly priest took a harmonica from his vest pocket and played a soulful rendition of "Going Home" as my mother's life slipped away. Maybe this was an unorthodox action, a spiritual form that is not in the books, but my rather traditional family deeply appreciated it. My father especially would tell the story afterward with gratitude and warmth.

Although many people today reject the word *religion* in favor of *spirituality,* religion, as a concrete, structured way of dealing with life's mysteries, is nevertheless important. If spirituality is left abstract, it doesn't address sick patients at an emotional and meaningful level. The genius of religious traditions has been to create rituals and symbols that speak powerfully to the heart as well as the head. Chaplains would be well advised to learn about symbol and ritual, and not only in traditional forms, so that they could both create concrete ways to speak to the spiritual needs of their patients and perceive the ritual nature of ordinary actions. The priest who played a song for my mother knew the power of music to mark a special moment, *the* special moment, in my mother's case.

I once lectured to students learning to be pastoral counselors and chaplains about the importance of ritual and their education in it. They looked at me as though I were speaking about something entirely irrelevant to them. To them, spirituality is about belief. Say the right words and you are in the proper spiritual place. They knew little, if anything, about the power of ritual and narrative and symbol to address a person's spiritual needs.

I recommended to these students the books of Mircea Eliade, the remarkable professor of religion and once head of the History of Religions program at the University of Chicago, who studied the basic forms that religion takes around the world and the themes that are essential to it. A chaplain would gain confidence by knowing the depth of the spiritual life—the essential symbols, the basic themes, and the images that come up again and again in religious traditions around the world.

I have already mentioned the theme of bread. This is essential in the Christian tradition as Eucharist, as the presentation of the very presence of Jesus. He himself had said, "I am the bread of life." But we also find something similar in the manna with which the Israelites were fed during their exodus. A study of spiritual traditions would teach a chaplain how to use water ritually and symbolically, how to shape prayer, and also how to prepare for an ordeal, such as surgery or chemotherapy. She would also recognize the deep meaning of a patient asking for a piece of bread in his dying days.

For too long we have practiced competition among religions rather than cooperation and commonality. Today we could learn much about the spiritual life by being less defensive and competitive. By studying the use of symbols common to the various traditions, we learn more about their meaning and how to use them in daily practice.

Yet, as rich as the traditions are, they don't tell the whole story. Spiritual insight can also be found in people who may never have had any connection to a religious or spiritual tradition. Secular writers, writing from the depth of their experience, may tell you more about the spirituality of illness than a textbook on the subject.

One day in the mid-1990s, I received a phone call from an editor at *The New York Times Book Review* asking for a review of a book on Jung. The man immediately impressed me with his voice, his diction, and the rich culture in his language and ideas. Anatole Broyard was later to make a further impression on me when he wrote a book during his treatment for prostate cancer, *Intoxicated by My Illness*. It is one of the most penetrating and beautiful books on illness I know.

He describes his first visit to a doctor to check on urinary problems. Sitting in the office, he noticed the fine furniture and studied the photographs on the desk, especially one of a sailboat. He concluded that this doctor "knew how to live—and by extension, how to look after the lives of others. His magic seemed good."[8]

The simple image of a sailboat gave some assurance to the patient about his doctor: a sailboat, an image of navigating the vagaries of wind and water currents and an image of life lived with daring and pleasure. The image, as Broyard read it, gave him confidence. How important are the images we put in healing environments. They are like statues and paintings in a church: they must be appropriate and potent and direct the attention of the patient toward his healing. The sailboat did just that for this highly literate man.

We ask much from doctors, and now I am asking them to be conscious and artful about the images they place in front of their patients. I am asking them to see beneath appearances and take note of spiritual meanings and developments. I am asking them to be spiritual guides and sacristans of a sort—people who are familiar with the objects and symbols that enhance the spiritual life.

Imagine a doctor observing the release of a patient's soul in a simple act of kindness and connecting it to her health and her capacity to die peacefully. Anatole Broyard says, "How can a doctor presume to cure a patient if he knows nothing about his soul, his personality, his character disorders? It's all part of it." He also makes a statement that is especially pleasing to me: "I used to get restless when people talked about soul, but now I know better. Soul is the part of you that you summon up in emergencies."

A chaplain is called to be a minister to the mysteries that surround a person's life, especially in illness. But anyone in the medical world is also called to attend people in their depths, when life becomes unusually multilayered and symbolic. Broyard says this perfectly: "I'd like my doctor to scan *me*, to grope for my spirit as well as my prostate."

In *Care of the Soul* I told the story of my cousin, who was a Servite sister and had lived her whole life in a religious order. She developed a mysterious illness and suffered from it for several years. She said she knew more about the sickness than any doctor she had found—she had been a science teacher and applied her knowledge to her disease.

She told me that one day, when she was lying in the hospital, feeling abandoned by her God and for the first time in her life without her trust and faith, a priest chaplain came into her room. She told him of her failure to find meaning and spiritual peace. His response was to run out the door. She told me that she couldn't forget the image of his back as he retreated. He didn't know how to handle a nun who had lost her faith.

The work of the chaplain is not easy. People have strong emotions, positive and negative, about their religion. Many are defensive about their beliefs, and many have conflicts created by their experience of religion. A representative of religion doesn't know how a person will react. He has to take time to get to know the patient to understand what is needed and what he can do. And today especially, he has to keep his mind open to all sorts of experiences people report to him in their illness.

Chaplains and pastoral counselors get extensive training in psychological theory and counseling techniques, but the most important resource they have, and the most difficult to prepare, is their own person. A counselor who has confronted herself and doesn't act out her biases and emotional conflicts can help a patient far more effectively than one who simply has learned the techniques. But modern medicine, with its sheen of technology and protocol, has influenced counselors' training and style. They are picking up some of its quick judgments, tendency to categorize, and limited notions of what is healthy. They might do better work if they offered a clear alternative to medicine's modernist leanings, if they drew on the traditions with imagination and creativity.

I once gave a talk at a large medical association in the South. I spoke for two and a half hours (with a break) about deepening spiritual, theological, and psychological ideas and learning about ritual and narrative for spiritual counseling in a hospital setting. In passing, I mentioned that followers of Jesus often make him into a stern and judgmental figure, whereas the Gospels present him as friendly and earthy. I referred to Gospels that were not included in the New Testament and noted that one, the Gospel of Philip, describes Jesus kissing Mary Magdalen.

The next day one of the professors told me that he had asked two of his students about my talk. They immediately complained of my reference to Jesus kissing Mary; they were outraged. He asked them, "You listened to many rich ideas about preparing yourself to be a spiritual counselor and all you can think of is a passing reference to Jesus kissing Mary?"

"Yes," they said.

The story struck me because it reminded me of how anxious spiritual people can be about sexuality. They try to make it less important in their lives, but then in daily life they are sensitive to the slightest reference to sex. If I were in an academic position, I would not pass a student in counseling who manifested so much sexual anxiety, and I would not want him counseling people in my hospital.

The larger issue is the need of chaplains and counselors to face their own demons and deal with their complexes as part of their preparation. Just as psychotherapists in general often include analysis or therapy as part of their training, chaplains and spiritual advisors could do the same and then do less harm in the hospital setting.

A Patient's Spiritual Journey Through Illness

Many years ago, while reading Mircea Eliade's journals, I came across his several references to illness as an initiation. He means "initiation" as a rite of passage, the transformation of a person, and a shift from one way of being to another. Illness is the means for a change in perception and can be the occasion for personal renewal.

In traditional, primal societies, initiations are elaborate and striking ceremonies. A young man or woman entering adult life may go through days of ritual involving body paint, masks, wild dances, piercing music, fasting, storytelling, and abandonment in the wilderness. All of these acts help the young person make a deeply felt shift in awareness, preparing him or her for a responsible life in the community.

Illness is not a mere ritual, obviously, but it does have qualities of an initiation. As a patient, you may feel abandoned and frightened, and may have to go through operations, tests, screenings, and hospitalizations that affect you profoundly. The symptoms of illness or the very idea of being seriously sick may give you thoughts of dying. Death is the main theme in initiation: death to an old life and rebirth into a new one. The focus on death and mortality during a serious illness may not be entirely literal but may offer a kind of death to the old person and an opportunity for new beginnings.

Eliade says of the illness a potential shaman often goes through: "The illness is the point of departure for the process of personality integration and for a radical spiritual transformation."[9] The same could be said of any patient lying in a hospital bed. His illness could be the point of departure for his spiritual transformation. After all, he is now at the edge of his existence. He can no longer enjoy the calming unconsciousness of ordinary life. Now he tastes his mortality and has to think about the meaning of his life, his basic values, and his very identity. He has to consider his past, his relationships, and the way he spends his time. Many people discover themselves on a hospital bed.

Many of the nurses and physiotherapists I interviewed for this book told me of the depression that usually settles on patients who have had traumatic injury that will prevent them from living their lives in the customary way. They are depressed because of their loss of function but also because they have to reassess who they are and the meaning of such a personal disaster for the rest of their lives. They are being initiated into a new life, one that they would not have chosen for themselves.

In another place in his journals Eliade goes further with his ideas on illness as initiation. He says that he would like to write a short book showing us how to "live in conformity with symbol, with the archetype. I'd insist on the function that the imagination has of spiritual technique, of fulfillment, equilibrium, and fecundation (well-known examples: those neurotics and psychotics who recover their health insofar as they succeed in regaining, through imagination, *the symbolism of their own body* . . .)."[10]

Notice here that Eliade is not talking about spirituality as a personal achievement in meditation or prayer, but as the enlargement of the imagination, especially seeing the illness in the largest possible terms. A man discovers that chronic stomach trouble signals the anger and outrage that he has swallowed instead of expressing. A woman finds that trouble with her feet says something about her resistance to walking out into the world with confidence.

I once had a student who complained of a chronic sore throat. Doctors, she said, told her that they couldn't find anything physically wrong with her. I talked with her for a long while and eventually she told me she felt as though there was broken glass in her throat. We discussed the glass, and she thought of it as her delicate self that had been smashed while growing up in a violent family setting. We set about restoring her sense of self and the precious glass vessel she knew herself to be, the symbolism of the body.

Once I worked with a sweet and gifted man who had trouble with serious obesity. He told me a dream in which he was sprawled out on the ground at the feet of a huge naked woman. From other aspects of his life, especially his extreme emotional attachments to women, I felt that he was in the thrall of the mother goddess, the one pictured in rough primitive sculptures as having huge breasts, thighs, and belly, the Great Mother. I wondered if his heavy body was a male version of the Venus of Willendorf, an image from 24,000–22,000 B.C.

A quite different spiritual malady that involves the body is anorexia. Women I have worked with who have this spiritual disease want to avoid being the Venus of Willendorf at all costs. They don't want flesh, food, or children. They have a profound need to aim for bodylessness, and that need can kill them.

These are spiritual and psychological issues expressed and symbolized by the body and specifically through its illness. The young woman had to restore her glass identity, and the man had to consider his enthrallment to Woman. In fact, both of them did explore the symbolism of their body illnesses and eventually came to a new level of being. The woman recovered her "voice" and made her needs and wishes known. The man found a way of relating that was not enthrallment but rather mutuality. The body is the soul.

Personal Spiritual Practice

James Wiggins is one of those extraordinary citizens quietly devoting his life to his local community. He was my professor in graduate school, where he inspired me in directions that were crucial to my later work. Now he is undergoing experimental treatment for chronic lymphocytic leukemia.

Dr. Wiggins heads an interfaith network in Syracuse, New York, and so I wrote and asked him about his experience with medicine: "What has helped you most to heal and deal with this disease?"

"The love and care of my wife and family is number one," he wrote. "The knowledge of so many other people thinking about and praying for my well-being is another significant factor—regardless of my own uncertainties about petitionary prayer, especially when I am not a praying person in traditional terms."

Dr. Wiggins makes an important point: You don't have to pray or include any spiritual practice in your healing in the usual ways. You don't have to prove that your prayer works. You don't have to worry about your skepticism or insult your intelligence by adopting spiritual practices that seem naïve to you. You can be spiritually intelligent and at the same time devout and humble, praying with the masses and appreciating whatever forms of prayer come your way.

I always say that I learned how to pray from my mother; her Catholicism was old-fashioned but intense and in its own way rigorously well informed. I don't share her worldview, but I would consider myself fortunate to achieve the level of spiritual integrity she enjoyed throughout her life.

A person facing illness has a deep emotional and relational life of family, spouse, children, friends, and relatives, but he or she also has a spiritual life, whether or not it is expressed in religious or other formal ways. One way for a patient to deal with his spiritual life is to invite the services of a chaplain or counselor. But there is much more that can be done.

A patient might place objects in his room that remind him of his spiritual values. One purpose of religion is memory, to help us call to mind our basic philosophy of life and the central figures and teachings that have shaped us. Because of my Catholic past, for instance, I would want a rosary and an image of the healing Jesus in my room. I'd also like images of Quan Yin, the healing goddess of Buddhism, simply because I find her so beautiful and comforting. I'd like a picture of the Lapis Lazuli Radiant Healing Buddha and a Sufi poem and a shaman's instrument—a drum, ladder, pipe, or flute. I'd like a collection of recorded music especially selected to keep me in a spiritual frame of mind.

I would meditate by lying calmly, doing nothing, between various medical activities or while waiting for a procedure or exam. I'd like to have someone read to me from sacred texts taken from various spiritual traditions. I would want some food that was natural and reminded me less of human processing and more of the bounty of nature.

It is probably too much to expect the kind of doctor that Anatole Broyard fantasizes: "He should be able to imagine the aloneness of the critically ill, a solitude as haunting as a Chirico painting. I want him to be my Virgil, leading me through my purgatory or inferno, pointing out the sights as we go."[11]

What Broyard is alluding to is the strong sensation, when you are seriously ill, that no matter how much your family and friends want to help, you are alone in your affliction and alone in facing your mortality. Psychological counseling can go only so far. It doesn't touch on the profound spiritual issues you face. You need someone—a doctor, nurse, or chaplain—who has the imagination to help you sort out the most difficult questions: Why me? What does it all mean and imply? Can I deal with dying? Can I say good-bye to loved ones? Has my life made sense? Has it all been worthwhile?

There are three kinds of people: religious, agnostic, and unconscious. Of course, this is a simplification. There are many varieties in between. But essentially people come to the spiritual crisis in illness through religion in some form.

Atheists and agnostics have their own brand of religion or non-religion. The passion with which they approach the matter of religion, usually critical and dismissive, often sounds similar to the passion of religious fundamentalists. Atheists and fundamentalists seem to be at opposite ends of a spectrum. I see an atheist's passion as a sincere effort to sort out the matter of religion and therefore as a highly spiritual activity in itself.

On a recent December weekend, I gave a retreat at a beautiful old building just outside Belfast in Northern Ireland. A young man was staying there with his family, but he wouldn't attend my talks because he was an atheist and was certain that I would offend his sensibilities. One evening we happened to sit next to each other at dinner and had a long conversation. As a result of our good connection, he started attending my presentations. I think he discovered that thoughtful atheism and thoughtful spirituality go together quite well.

Whether you are a pious believer, an atheist, or somewhere in between, you still have an important resource in your spirituality as you deal with illness. You can always look deep into yourself for strength. You can always surrender to the "will" of life. You can always hope and even pray in your own way, reaching beyond yourself, even if you don't have any notion of a beyond.

I spend a portion of every year in Ireland, and there, in the year 2000, I met John Moriarty, a man I consider the best writer Ireland has produced since Samuel Beckett—and there is a lot of competition for that honor. John was always spilling over with ideas and language and emotion. Some thought he was too ebullient in his writing and in his presentations, but I enjoyed his excess. We met for the first time in a hotel just off Grafton Street, the pedestrian-friendly, car-free avenue lined with shops and restaurants in the heart of Dublin. We intended to have a brief chat but ended up spending hours drinking tea in a quiet loggia of the hotel. We became good friends, and when I returned to the United States—I was living in Dublin when I met John—we continued to write and talk on the phone.

Seven years after that meeting in Dublin, John called me to inform me that he had cancer of the lungs, the liver, and, as people might say in Ireland, the bowel. He became anxious and depressed, and he told me how low he had sunk into despair over his illness. He went on the radio, which in Ireland amounts to addressing a good part of the population. He bared his soul and publicly announced his despair. He said he had been given a death sentence.

But a year later I happened to be in Dublin the day John was getting an experimental treatment that represented his last chance at a cure. I went to the hospital to visit him. When I got to his room, I saw him lying on his side, asleep. I wondered how he might be feeling now. I returned in an hour and found him awake and looking surprisingly healthy. He had lost weight and had trimmed his hair. We sat and talked theology, laughed about past experiences, and discussed his spiritual state. He had turned a corner. He was now ready to die. His anxiety and depression had gone. When I stood up to leave, he asked me for a blessing. I made the sign of the cross over him, placed my hand on his head, and said the words of blessing in Latin, knowing that he would appreciate that. Two months later he died.

John knew myth and sacred literature and theology better than anyone I have ever known, and yet he went through difficult phases in his spiritual experience of a fatal illness. He had faced many hardships in his life and step by step his spirituality broadened and deepened. You can read the tale in his many books. But cancer put him on the edge as never before. At first, it threw him. He didn't know how to react. But then gradually he came to see what was happening to him. He found meaning.

At the end John used words that people sometimes draw on to express the peace they have found. He said to me, "I no longer ask 'Why me?' Now I ask, 'Why not me?'"

In serious illness, psychology and spirituality come together. Meaning and emotion. Hope and courage. Vision and understanding. Psychology is not sufficient. A spiritual point of view is needed to see beyond your fears and to transcend your personal concerns. You connect with a great world, and, paradoxically, in your solitude you find commonality with others who have faced death with wonder and expectation.

James Wiggins made a point that is crucial. "I truly believe," he wrote to me, "that a positive way of living one's life contributes to recovering from illness, if recovery is possible." I would add that the way you live your life also makes it possible to deal with a terminal illness with courage and calm, even if, as in the case of John Moriarty, you have to go through a tunnel of discovery before the calm.

One day we will all receive the bad news that our body is seriously breaking down. How we receive that news and how we deal with it depends in large measure on how well we have tended our soul and spirit.

PART II

THE SOULFUL HEALER

*Our physician is in us and everything
we need is within our nature.*

— PARACELSUS, *OPUS PARAMIRUM* 6.13

CHAPTER 5

BAD NEWS

I was walking the streets of Seattle one day, not the steep avenues up from the water, but the flat ones. I had gone several blocks and had reached the center of downtown and was standing on a corner waiting for a traffic light to change when suddenly I thought I might pass out. My head got light and fuzzy and I stumbled. I stood still for a few minutes and returned to normal. I didn't do any more extensive walking on that trip.

When I returned home to New Hampshire, I delayed a few days and then made an appointment with my doctor. He looked concerned and immediately set up a stress test. I didn't think it was my heart, but I didn't do well on the test. The cardiologist, Dr. Kalra, whom I've already discussed, asked me to see him a few days later and asked my wife to come along. Never had a doctor asked me to come for an appointment with my wife.

We sat with him in his small office and he told me that I had heart disease. He assured me that he and his colleagues could take care of it. Still, I felt my mortality crash down from the sky onto my head. I didn't panic, but later, while waiting two weeks for treatment, I did become depressed.

In my view there are many kinds of depression. This one seemed to be the kind that comes from a visitation of Death. Suddenly nothing about life looked the same. I felt depressed because I could no longer be the youthful person I had been. I thought of my wife, 15 years younger than me. I didn't want to be an old, invalid husband. I thought of my children, 15 and 12 at the time. I didn't want to leave them yet.

Gradually, as the angioplasty drew near, I gained some hope. The morning of the procedure, my wife and I got up in early November darkness and drove an hour to the hospital. Nurses and attendants prepped me, and the doctor came to my bed and said that because of the position of the blockage he didn't know if the angioplasty would work. He couldn't promise anything. Suddenly I sank back into anxiety and a shallow depression. What if it didn't?

I understand that my condition, serious as it was, is quite common and perhaps is not as overwhelmingly threatening as a diagnosis of cancer. I even tried to think of it as not so serious, all the time knowing that it was indeed, and still is, life-threatening. My diagnosis was bad news, and my off-and-on depression was, as I see it, an appropriate response.

My depression served me. It guided me to a place where I had to make a serious evaluation of my life and have some unusually poignant conversations with my family. It goaded me to contact friends who could offer suggestions and professional help. I called my friend Dr. Balfour Mount in Montreal, a professor of medicine at McGill University. He told me to trust myself to the experts on this one. I got in touch with Dr. Herbert Benson at Harvard University, the author of the classic book *The Relaxation Response*. He offered his help but most of all advised me to meditate and relax deeply. I spoke with my close friend Dr. Bettina Peyton, who advised me about local cardiologists. My friends gave me largely practical advice, but just contacting them and relying on them during this episode healed me of my usual excessive self-reliance.

Depression and anxiety can be useful. They turn the mind in a certain direction and give you the emotional impetus to do what needs to be done. You have to allow them to settle in and affect you. You can't always be looking for ways to get rid of them or make little of them. You need the big imagination that goes against the spirit of the times. Today people want constant equilibrium. They want every day to be a normal one.

In a hotel on one of my trips I was watching the weather map on television. The forecast was for ice storms in many states. The reporter concluded her report by saying, "Everyone wants to know when life will return to normal." *Yes*, I thought. In general, today everyone faced with an emergency or inconvenience wants to know when life will return to normal. This sentiment is a key element in the philosophy of our time.

But normal often means unconscious. To return to normal means to go back to the state of numbness when we don't have to think about things. Sometimes it's beneficial to be shaken up and cast out of the Eden of our mindlessness. We get back into life and return our focus to the things that matter.

Bad News as Initiation

We have already discussed how illness can be an initiation or rite of passage. Getting bad news about our health can be a particularly potent nudge into consciousness, an impetus toward transformation. It is a brief but penetrating piece of the overall rite of passage that embraces the discovery of symptoms, the news from the doctor, the plan of treatment, the procedures, and the aftermath.

In fact, hearing bad news about our health may not be so brief. It is told in a few minutes, usually, but the impact lingers and colors every other stage of the illness. How it is presented and what we do with it make all the difference.

Let's start with the point of view of the health-care worker—usually the doctor or surgeon. How to break bad news comes up in the training of nurses and doctors, and many experienced experts have developed guidelines. I'd like to offer my own.

First, attitude is important. Pity, distance, and superiority give a negative charge to delivering bad news. The health-care worker may feel, "You're sick and I'm not." The patient picks up on this silent message and feels worse. Doctors and nurses might remember, especially in these crucial moments with patients, that they, too, are susceptible to disease and organ malfunctioning. We all get sick and we all die. It's an obvious observation, but it can be repressed as a way of fending off the professional's own mortality.

In archetypal psychology, we talk about a "split archetype." This is an unfortunate emotional pattern that may characterize the relationship between a health-care professional and a patient. In the best of circumstances, the professional is aware that we all get sick and die. He is aware that he and the patient share a common humanity and both are susceptible to illness. For his part, the patient doesn't give full authority and control over to the professional. He studies his illness and makes decisions about it. Together, patient and doctor keep the archetype intact, both connected to the role of healer and patient.[12] A doctor might make the common bond explicit: "I've had heart surgery, and I know how it feels to be told you're sick." We don't usually encourage psychotherapists to talk about their own problems, but it's different with a doctor.

Before delivering bad news, the professional might take stock and notice what his fears and resistance are about. What comes up in him at the thought of giving a person bad medical news? What is it about this particular patient?

He can also consider his strengths. He may be a good conversationalist. He may have a positive view of life that will help his patient. He may be confident that something can be done.

Guidelines for delivering bad news often recommend finding an appropriate place. A busy corridor or a waiting room full of patients may not be the best setting. People need privacy at these moments. My cardiologist's bad news was not as sensitive as some might be, but even so I appreciated being in a small private office when he spoke to me and my wife.

Privacy itself is a big issue in medicine, not only keeping records confidential but also guarding a patient's personal privacy in a hospital or doctor's office. We comment on how illness makes us feel alone with our fate, but we don't often take the next step and protect the privacy of the patient. Especially in shared rooms, there are circumstances when an important private moment may be shattered.

The professional's tone of voice, too, colors his words significantly. Are you preoccupied with something else? Trying too hard to be understanding? Distracted? Bothered? Anxious? Are these feelings getting into your voice and giving a message that is a counterpoint to your intentions? Your emotions have to be in tune with your message. You may be giving the required information to a distressed patient and family member, but underneath it you're saying: "I'm telling you the facts of the case, but I don't have time to hold your hand and massage your emotions." The underlying message is often more powerful than the intended one.

What follows is a list of rules I offered a group of nurses for delivering bad news:

- Be as clear and as honest as possible without gory details.

- Don't start out as though you're going to give a death sentence, speaking from your own anxiety and foreboding and showing your worry. Go straight to the message.

- Offer any and all hope possible.

- If there is no hope, offer extraordinary measures of support: "I'm available." "We have a great staff." "Counselors are here." "Many people in your situation do well." "We can make you comfortable." "We will welcome your family."

- Ask: "Is there anything you don't understand? Anything you want to know? Anything you'd like to say?"

Miracles happen. Norman Cousins ended his book *Anatomy of an Illness,* in which he describes how he was given a death sentence and cured himself with laughter and a positive attitude, with the story of a chance meeting on a street with his doctor of doom. He shook the doctor's hand. "I increased the pressure until he winced and asked to be released." The doctor wanted to know how Cousins had recovered. "It all began, I said, when I decided that some experts don't really know enough to make a pronouncement of doom on a human being."[13]

A miracle is not necessarily a surprise release from the laws of nature. It may be a cure created by a good mental attitude or a supportive family. It could even be the result of the extraordinary skill of a surgeon. We should keep our definition of *miracle* open and less naïve than usual.

When you give bad news, the possibility of a miracle may not be wishful thinking but rather a broad idea of what can cure. Certainly, offering a pessimistic view under the aegis of realism and honesty may prevent the miracle of a cure.

The Obfuscating Language of Medicine

Obfuscate is one of those words that does what it means—to make difficult. It comes from a Latin word meaning "dark color" or "brown." We hope that language will enlighten us and the people we're talking to, but often it "endarkens." Medical language certainly obfuscates many an attempt to communicate.

Many of the words used in medicine are either in Latin or derived from Latin or sometimes Greek—dementia, delirium, bacteria, pneumonia, angina pectoris, schizophrenia, tibia, femur, and hypoglycemia. The average person finds it nearly impossible to pronounce certain basic drugs. Try alpha-methylthiofentanyl or piperidinocyclohexanecarbonitrile. "Acute viral rhinopharyngitis, or acute coryza . . . is a contagious, viral infectious disease of the upper respiratory system, primarily caused by picornaviruses (including rhinoviruses) or coronaviruses"—this is an opening sentence from the Wikipedia article on the common cold.

People often wonder if the arcane language of medicine serves the purpose of a secret code, keeping the club of doctors remote and sealed. Certainly it makes communication between patients and doctors difficult and keeps them separated into two alien worlds. Health-care workers could make an effort to speak more clearly to patients.

One February I joined a group of doctors in Jackson Hole, Wyoming, where the temperature reached 14 degrees below zero, to discuss something called "health literacy." I thought it might be an effort to break down the barriers between doctors and patients by finding new ways to educate and speak to them. But as part of the program we watched a film that showed how ignorant laypeople are about medical matters. The implication was that professionals need to talk down to them more than they do already.

Only a few doctors present took issue with the direction of the seminar and suggested that doctors need to be more human and connect with their patients better. They need to be present as persons more than they need to lower the level of their language.

Of course, any field or discipline of study will have its own vocabulary and technical terminology. A layman would find it difficult reading Freudian literature, or even reading about plumbing, for that matter. But medicine is a special case. There, the arcane nature of the vocabulary goes far beyond the reasonable, and it is a significant issue given the importance of communication between doctor and patient.

As a writer, I notice another problem in medical literature. Essays on specific issues often break all the rules of good writing. In particular, medical writing is full of passive voice and nominalizations, anathema to good style. The following is from an abstract published by a major university press: "The value of measuring age, blood pressure, weight, smoking habits, exercise and serum cholesterol in predicting death and coronary heart disease was studied over a period of ten years. Sixteen groups comprising 12,763 men aged 40–59 years (at the outset) from seven countries (Yugoslavia, Finland, Italy, The Netherlands, Greece, USA and Japan) were studied. The highest risk factors were found to be age, systolic blood pressure, and serum cholesterol concentration (related to saturated fatty acids in the diet). Differences in incidence rates could not be shown to be related to characteristics of the cohorts in relative body weight, smoking habits or physical activity. The methods of handling the data will be of particular interest to epidemiologists."

In this paragraph, every sentence uses passive voice. One sentence contains an ingenious double passive: "could not be shown to be related." "Characteristics of the cohorts" employs a nice alliteration, but I have no idea what it means. Health literacy could begin with doctors learning how to express themselves more clearly—fewer passives and more verbs. My sense in reading technical essays written in atrocious style is that the authors are betraying the mechanistic philosophy that long ago invaded medicine. We treat the body as a machine and then talk about it mechanically. You could imagine a robot talking this way.

Passive voice is a way of taking the subject out of a statement. My teenage daughter has a telephone message, pre-recorded from the communications company, that says, "Please listen to the music while your party is reached." No subject. Cold and mechanical. Trying to sound officious. It's the same with medicine. We take the subjects, the people, out of the equation and deal with objects. Our language betrays the style in which we think of medicine and practice it.

Peering further into the robot-like language of medicine, we glimpse one of the deepest problems in modern culture, a failure to value beauty and style. As long as our language works, we are satisfied. Many highly educated people never think about style or the rules of writing or the goal of beauty in expression. In general, medicine has failed to appreciate the place of the beautiful in the treatment of sick people, and this failure shows up in doctor-patient conversations and in professional journals.

You see the absence of beauty in hospital rooms and physicians' examining rooms. Our entire medical experience would be transformed if we gave beauty serious consideration in every aspect of care. The ancient Greeks would say that we offend the spirit of Aphrodite, goddess of beauty, and their plays warn us that when Aphrodite is scorned, she seeks her revenge.

Beauty and style in expression are gifts of this spirit that has been neglected too often by those dedicated to the myth of modernism. We seem to love our obtuseness and are impressed with language that is unintelligible except to the elite and initiated. But the payoff for this hiding behind professionalism is a weakening of the healing contract between patient and health-care worker.

The soul opens up in the ambience of the beautiful. People gain hope and want life in its fullness. When the style of healing lacks beauty, all that is left is the skill of the doctor and technician, and these are not enough to inspire the full participation of the patient in the process of getting better. Attention to the way doctors and other professionals speak and write could bring more humanity to the practice of medicine.

Messenger of Mortality

A doctor or nurse often has to play the role of messenger of death. It is an archetypal, mythic role that has deep roots. It demands spiritual fortitude from both the messenger and the patient. In Greek tragedy, a messenger often appears to announce bad news that gives the story a sharp turn in a challenging direction.

I noticed that when my mother quickly, overnight, went from a happy and healthy housewife to a patient in brain surgery, my father resisted the emotional defense of sentimentality. He phoned to ask my advice about a key decision he had to make. Should he allow her to go through brain surgery or should he let her die immediately and peacefully?

He told me that we had about three minutes to make the decision. I was at my home in New Hampshire. He was in the Detroit area, a thousand miles away. How could I make the decision to let my mother die? I asked him if she had expressed her will. "Yes," he said, "she said minutes ago that she wanted a chance to live."

"Is there a chance that she could come out of this?"

"Yes," he said, "but it's not a good chance, and I don't want her to be in a vegetable condition."

"What do you think, Dad?" I asked.

"I think we should let her go."

"I can't say that. If she has expressed her desire for a chance to live and there is some possibility, I think we should allow it."

"Okay," he said immediately. "We'll operate."

Two years later, during a quiet conversation in his home, my father said to me, "I think we should have let her go." My mother did have about two months of relative clarity after her surgery, before dementia began to set in. But soon she lost her memory and her personality changed. I never knew how much of her confusion was caused by the heavy drugs she was given. I tried many times to have the drugs lessened but succeeded only after weeks of effort. She kept getting weaker and her capacity kept diminishing until she died peacefully. I'm still happy that we made the decision we did, but my father was with my mother the entire time of her dying. He knows the suffering she went through.

My father has told me that he is relying on me to make tough decisions about him. He doesn't want any effort made to keep him alive. He's 96 and has lived a good life. He wants me to be strong in the face of bad news. His underlying message, conveyed to me many times: no sentimentality.

On the other hand, a friend of mine, Charlotte Parker, with her sister Virginia, has written a touching book on living with her mother's dementia. It is about a family "that consciously chose to step into their demented mother's reality, as opposed to forcing her to live in a world in which she no longer belonged."[14] Similarly, while in his 90s, my father worked for several years as an advocate for dementia patients, entering their reality with great respect and effectiveness.

Facing death through illness can sometimes push you to the very edge of your understanding and emotional strength. Because of my work in medicine, I have met several mothers who have young children and who have cancer without much or any hope of survival. "What can I do?" they ask.

What can they do but cultivate a deep faith in life? Trust that their children will get along with surviving family members. Have faith that this tragic development, unwanted and hardly tolerable, could be a catalyst for an especially intense and creative life. What is left but pure and undemanding love? And at the end of the struggle for meaning, there is a sliver of hope. Faith, hope, and charity—these three classic virtues are so easy to recite and promote but so difficult to live in the context of bad news.

These virtues don't arrive without effort and cost. They don't come immediately upon the arrival of the news of the illness. First there may be denial, bartering, depression, hysteria, anger, and collapse. But these apparently negative responses may all be the building blocks of deep faith. Faith is the result of a process, not an instant achievement.

A person who has had a naïve view of faith all his life may now, in the face of mortality, have to discover a different kind of faith. Not childish belief that a miracle will cure him, but faith in the entire story of his life, including his final disease. Not faith as belief in a story that is merely traditional, but faith as trust in life itself. Not faith as unquestioning assent to what others have told him, but profound trust in his family and friends and even in the health-care givers who offer their lives for his well-being.

The health-care worker who deals with these impossible, heart-wrenching experiences of dying and leaving loved ones behind somehow has to know all this and have the capacity to be part of it.

When as a professional or family member you have to deal with death, keep your mind open. Don't expect a certain response and certainly don't demand a particular response that you might approve. Stay open. Allow for a wide range of responses. Take them in. When you respond yourself, offer not advice but adequate information. Know that your patient or loved one will have to go through several phases. Don't be afraid. Allow this person's struggle a place in your heart. You will be a better person and professional because of it.

CHAPTER 6

HEALTH CARE: A JOB OR A CALLING?

It's a fine spring morning in Hartford. I'm looking forward to the busy day because we are going to interview residents, young men and women who have completed their basic medical training and are now attached to the hospital for further experience, education, and supervision. Intentionally we have scheduled them for the lunch period, knowing that the young always appreciate free food, and they arrive with high energy, carrying notepads and books and proudly wearing stethoscopes around their necks, the ritual sign of their advanced status as doctors.

Mark McKinney, Sharon O'Brien, and I tell them that we have been touring the hospital for months, trying to unearth the human side of medical practice and even the soul of the hospital. One young man looks up, interested, and wants to talk. Most of the others look more closely at their sandwiches or go back to texting on their cell phones. One responds to a beeper and rushes out the door.

It's clear that these are busy people. They are being asked to study, learn, observe, and practice medicine during long days with little sleep and a challenging social life. Who has time to talk about the soul of medicine? But they are generally civil and somewhat attentive, though they look eager to dart toward the door once the allotted hour is over.

From the limited conversation, I get the impression that these young doctors have by now been profoundly indoctrinated. They believe in the science of medicine and probably haven't had occasion to discuss the art of medicine. They seem to be on the cusp between feeling the call to heal sick people and the job of being a modern doctor.

I talk to them about their calling. Oh yes, they remember once feeling a deep desire to be there for people in need of expert medical attention. Some of them talk about their mothers and fathers, also doctors, who inspired them. Then they discuss the erosion of their ideals in years of demanding technical studies and the attitude of many depressed and overworked doctors who taught them.

The Beauty of a Calling

Some people hear the word *calling* and think of something supernatural, mystical, and magical. Some think of Saint Paul being knocked off a horse. But a calling may be powerful without being so literally otherworldly. You won't be kicked out of the driver's seat of a car, but you may feel stunned by the potency of your imagination of what you could be.

Let's keep *calling* in the passive voice—you are called. You may even hear actual voices; those of friends, teachers, and mentors, saying something so important to you that you change your life because of it.

Just a few years after I left the monastery, I was taking classes at the University of Windsor in Ontario. I was studying theology, but I had no intention of working on behalf of a church or even a particular religion. I was interested in religion as such and not as a belief system. I was in reaction against the religious life I had lived intensely for a dozen years or more.

One day a professor whom I liked very much, Lonnie Kliever, told me he thought I should study for a doctorate in religion. "No way," I said. "I've had enough of church for a while."

"You could study religion more openly without any worry about belief or organization at Syracuse University," he said. The University of Windsor did not have a doctoral program in religious studies.

He had made the overture to me, and suddenly I heard his words as some sort of pronouncement for myself. I followed up on his suggestion and ultimately found my calling at Syracuse. Yes, this was a second calling for me. Previously I had felt strongly called to the priesthood, but now I felt energized and focused. I studied hard and developed a life work out of my years studying religion in a new way.

A calling is not just a job. You feel invited to do a certain kind of work that will give your life meaning. You give your all to it and are willing to go to extremes to prepare yourself, as I did by spending 13 years in a seminary. You arrange your life around your work and find pleasure in what you are doing. People engaged in a calling, rather than a mere job, often say that they would do the work even if they weren't paid. Or they say that it doesn't feel like work. That is because the reward is inherent in the work itself and not in the money or prestige the work offers.

Doctors or nurses who still feel the work as a calling will more easily be present to their patients and bring more attention to the details of their work. They may work long hours willingly because the work gives them a sense of meaning. Because of it, their lives are worthwhile. They apply themselves to their work with special vigor because it is the meaning of their lives, and their patients perceive this passion and engagement easily. It radiates from them, defining them and giving their work much of its potency.

In his fascinating book on being a surgeon, *The Scalpel and the Soul*, Allan J. Hamilton tells the story of a revered medical professor at Harvard, Dr. Judah Folkman, being invited to give a convocation address for the medical school. "Is there a doctor in the house?" he asked a roomful of medical professionals. Dr. Hamilton comments, "He meant the physician in whom you put your trust and your life. So as we looked at one another in bewilderment on that quadrangle, we wondered who among us would become doctors and who among us would remain M.D.s—technicians only."[15]

Here is another way of putting it: Are you a doctor or a technician? Do you have a calling that you feel, or are you just doing your job? If it's a job you're doing, you may not be really seeing your patients, and they may not be really feeling your presence, which is precious to them. If it is only a job for you, you will probably burn out quickly or become depressed or cynical or distant. A calling touches your soul, while a mere job only reaches as far as your wallet and your professional standing.

I don't want to exaggerate the idea of calling. You won't love every minute of your work just because you realize that it's your calling. But you will be fully involved and present. You will sense the response of your patients and co-workers, and that response will sustain you. You will probably do your work better, because you are so involved and interested. A sense of calling can make all the difference.

Nurses have a special calling. They are drawn to close contact with patients, healing through constant, intimate care rather than chiefly through skill and knowledge. This is not to say at all that nurses do not need or have skills and education. In fact, every day they take over more of the jobs previously restricted to physicians. But what distinguishes their work from that of doctors, for all its professionalism, is their ongoing, constant, and close relationship with patients. You could say that among their skills is an interpersonal connection that inspires and supports a patient through a variety of treatments and through a succession of successes and setbacks.

Often, when teaching and lecturing to psychotherapists, I mention that the word *therapy* comes from the Greek word *theraps*, meaning "attendant" and, by extension, "nurse." When I consider nurses and the important work they do, I reverse that observation. Nurses are therapists, healers, caretakers of body, soul, and spirit. I never tire of quoting Plato's *Euthyphro*, where in the voice of Socrates he says that therapy means service to the gods. I take this to mean caring for people who are ill when the deep mysteries of human existence press, threaten, and challenge. A health-care worker is doing a special, spiritual task. His work is his vocation.

It may seem strange to put it this way, but a patient has a calling, too. When an illness presents itself to us, we are called to a new task, to the challenges and requirements of being healed and eventually dying. Some people refuse the call and pretend to be on a mere excursion from normal life.

Illness doesn't offer the choice of whether to be healthy or sick, but it does present an alternative for dealing with a new life. Today a patient can study his illness and participate actively in his treatment. He can take the lead in dealing with the emotional, relational, and spiritual aspects of his illness. He can discuss his treatment and consider alternatives and additions. He can help his family and loved ones deal with their worry. The patient has a lot of work to do, and that work might be easier if he understood it as yet another calling in life.

How Do You Educate for a Calling?

A calling often shows itself quite early in a person's life, and so parents and teachers can help nurture it. The method is obvious: You see signs of a child's interests and you encourage her in that direction. You're careful to distinguish between what you would have wanted for yourself and what you see in this child. You don't force your own wishes and values onto her. You understand that a life calling reveals itself over time and may take many turns. You don't know at first exactly what this person could become. Jonas Salk's mother thought he would become a lawyer, but she nurtured his confidence to the point that he could eventually become a brilliant medical researcher.

In school, a good teacher notices the strengths and weaknesses of a student and doesn't just brand him a failure if he doesn't succeed in a certain direction. He also knows that it isn't always easy to be specific about indications toward a life work. Albert Schweitzer, for example, who spent decades in Africa at his simple hospital, seems to have been called more to respond to human need in general than to a life in medicine. He told stories of his childhood, when he was especially sensitive to the suffering of people and animals that led to his personal philosophy of "reverence for life." He was called to offer that reverence and did so as a remarkably successful musician, writer, theologian, and doctor. He was truly a healer of souls.

During your education you nurture a calling by keeping it in mind, by not allowing all the technical details of training to obscure the deep reason for being in medicine in the first place, and by choosing specialties and courses according to the deep and lasting passion rather than according to what is expedient. You use your calling as a rudder while you navigate the complex sea of challenges. You keep referring back to your initial inspiration, and in that way your education in medicine has soul.

You will be tempted to go for the money, the success, and the prestige. You will be ridiculed if you suggest that you have a calling and that that is the important thing. You may be called a dreamer, a New Age idealist, or a sentimentalist.

Schweitzer decided at one point not to be susceptible to the charge of sentimentality, which is sometimes confused with passion. Modernism is not sentimental. It prefers cold facts to warm attachments and ideals. It likes a sober mind that doesn't fall for things like destiny, intuition, and callings.

But it's time to shed modernist values that are tired and have revealed their limitations. Today, in the 21st century, we can be professional and idealist at the same time. We can be spiritual without being obnoxiously ideological. We can see our life work as a calling without being naïve and over-emotional.

You can follow through on your calling by giving yourself a somewhat individualized education based on what you know to be your nature and inclination. It isn't always easy to do this in a medical setting, and so the choices may have to be small and subtle. But even the slightest attention to your calling keeps it in your mind and active in your work. As long as you remain cognizant of your calling, your work will have a foundation for soul, and that is no small achievement.

A calling to a life work is dynamic, not static. It may change significantly at various turning points in life, or it may just shift in small increments. It may have to do with additions or subtractions in the work you do. Several years ago I had a precancerous lesion removed from my face, and during the procedure the highly skilled plastic surgeon told me how he had joined a group of doctors who go to undeveloped countries a few times each year to operate on cleft lips. This extra service meant a great deal to the doctor and seemed to complete his calling to medicine.

Twists and Turns

A calling may not endure for the entire course of a life. You may reach a point where you want to move in a different direction, or you may do your work in medicine and find your calling elsewhere.

Some time ago I had a friend who had been a dentist for many years. I met him in his role of directing a men's choir in a local church. You couldn't help but be overwhelmed by the enthusiasm he brought to his work with the choir. He spent hours arranging, composing, and printing out music and then rehearsing it with the dozen or so men, who adored him. He welcomed me into their group and performed many of my compositions over a period of years. The choir was one of those societies that become the center of your life, even though you have more important things to do.

I wondered if my friend really had a calling to music and might consider leaving dentistry to become a full-time musician. But one day I went to him for my own dental needs and discovered that he brought the same passion and interest to his work as a dentist. I saw that he had two callings and that neither had to outrun the other.

Since then I have met many health-care workers who live a double life. They are completely involved in their medical professions, but they also work seriously in an art, craft, or other activity. One is a photographer. Another writes fiction. Yet another is a serious meditator. It is possible to have more than one calling and to be fulfilled and enriched in several kinds of activity, even if one dominates as the source of income.

It's useful to think of these activities as callings so that you take them seriously and understand how important they are to you. You come to them with your passion and eagerness. You give them as much time as you can, and you become good at the various things you do.

Some activities lie outside the boundary of a calling. I play golf for my heart and for some pleasure, but I'm so bad at it that I would never dignify it with the word *calling*. It's an avocation. If I have time for it, that's satisfying.

But if I have to forego some games because of more important engagements, it doesn't worry me. On the other hand, we all know people who live for golf and design their lives around the game.

You may have multiple callings that come into place one after the other. Serial callings. I met a man once who was a good psychiatrist. He had gone through extensive education and worked at a job that he enjoyed. I met him when he came to a class I was giving as a form of professional continuing education. But, he told me, what he really wanted to do and what he dreamed about constantly was to become an actor. His passion for acting was so intense, I wondered if he could continue his good work in medicine if he didn't give acting a chance. Maybe he could manage to do both, or maybe it was time to switch from one calling to another.

Let's return to Albert Schweitzer. He was an accomplished musician, writer, and theologian. He had made his mark in all three of these endeavors. Yet he felt that to really do the work he was called to do, he would have to study medicine and become a doctor. As the world knows, he did become a doctor and founded a hospital in a needy part of Africa. His life reveals yet another version of serial callings.

My father's life offers an extraordinary example, in a simple life, of major shifts in calling. He started out as a plumber, working with his father on commercial projects in Detroit. Then he was given the opportunity to teach plumbing in a trade school in the city. A born teacher, he took the job immediately and spent his life teaching. He retired at 62 and said he thought he would live a dozen years longer collecting stamps and relaxing. But then, when he was 90, my mother died, and he saw an opportunity to do some good and enjoy himself volunteering at the hospital where she had been in her last few months. He became an advocate and navigator for Alzheimer's and dementia patients and worked at the job for four years. His life centered on this work, which had all the earmarks of a genuine calling. He quit the work at 96 because he didn't think it was safe for him any longer to drive the three miles to the hospital.

When you visit a hospital, you will come across volunteers who find meaning in helping others in times of distress. They may not be making money, but they are fulfilling a seed buried deep in them that is the same seed that moved Albert Schweitzer to study medicine and move to Africa. It isn't about making money or being a star. These people understand that the best way to find meaning for yourself and make your life worth living is to become empty of any remaining self-absorption by doing service.

This, too, is part of a calling. It involves doing work that you would do even if you didn't get paid for it. It takes you to a place where you offer your service to others regardless of the rewards to you. By focusing on your contribution to community, rather than pay, you get more of what you need to feel fulfilled. Interviewing nurses, I listened to many say that they often stay late at work because their job is not mainly about a paycheck, although money is important. What really matters is caring for their patients.

Nurses and doctors describe this kind of dedication in matter-of-fact tones. They see nothing heroic in it. It is their life work, and to the extent that it is possible they give it their time and energy.

Nurses did say that an expression of gratitude is important when the pay is not the issue. They deeply appreciate a card or letter or a simple "Thank you" from a patient. Patients and families may look on the nurses as simply doing their jobs and may not realize how important an expression of gratitude is to someone who is going beyond the call of duty. The health-care worker operates from a sense of calling rather than the demands of the occupation and in return needs a human response.

People in medical circles often complain of burnout and look for a psychological solution for it. I think that a better solution is social. We all need recognition and gratitude for the efforts we make on behalf of others, even if those efforts are part of our job and we get paid for them. Simple civility requires that we thank each other and express our appreciation. I have no doubt that this is a lesson that doctors badly need to learn in relation to nurses, but it is one that patients and their families should learn as well. Gratitude and appreciation should never go unspoken, and there is no need to understate them.

The Spirituality of a Calling

Looking on a medical career as a calling rather than just a job raises the work to the level of a spiritual activity. Remember that spirituality has to do with transcendence, and going beyond oneself in motivation and dedication is a way to transcend. Being aware of a calling to contribute to community places your work in a spiritual context, because community involvement is an important dimension of spirit.

Graduations, commencements, parties, certificates, traditional initiation rites—they can all help draw attention to the spiritual dimension. I met a woman once who told me that in preparation for her life as a doctor, she had decided to be celibate for two years. She said that her friends thought she was out of her mind, but I understood her idea completely and supported her in it. It is traditional in spiritual communities to mark a major shift in level or responsibilities by abstaining from some desirable object— food, entertainment, or sex.

The philosophy of modernism doesn't appreciate the importance of ritual and image. It allows subtle instances, usually vestiges of old rituals, but with reservations. A young doctor may make much of wearing a stethoscope around her neck or put on a white coat as a sign of her station. I could imagine a medical school offering a weeklong retreat led by appropriate spiritual guides or a dinner dedicated to the vocation in medicine. But imagine a medical school arranging for a vision quest or a period of celibacy and fasting before graduation. Serious spiritual practices in medicine are still a ways off.

Those nurses who said that they would do the work even if they weren't paid for it were expressing a valid and important point: there is a dimension of the work that goes far beyond payment in money. At the same time, they find more joy in their work now that they are paid better than in the past. Money is a significant way in which the community acknowledges the value of medical service. It is also the reason why many doctors are thinking about moving to another profession, chiefly because of the business side of their practices: dealing with insurance companies, facing malpractice lawsuits, and spending more time on money than on people.

As always, money is a mixed blessing. It adds a dimension to a calling in medicine that has both a negative and a positive impact. As government and businesses look for ways to pay for expensive medical care, health-care workers try to sort out issues of calling from the desire to make a good living. Each has a place, and the goal is to give both calling and money consideration while making career decisions in medicine.

When visionary people discuss spirituality in medicine, they often overlook this important issue of vocation. They don't seem to realize that when workers feel called to medicine, they have a different attitude toward their work and their patients than if they are only doing a job. In a vestigial way, they are bringing back the role of spiritual healer you find in traditional societies and in earlier periods of history, and that role is the best foundation for bringing soul and spirit to medicine.

CHAPTER 7

HEALING DREAMS AND IMAGES

When I go to see my current cardiologist, whom I admire and appreciate, I go through the usual rituals that I have already mentioned: dealing with the receptionist and insurance forms, reading old magazines, listening for my name to be called, and finally waiting in the examining room for the doctor to appear.

Each time I'm led into the little room, I find myself a little nervous and in the company of a plastic model of a diseased heart. I notice the unnatural coloring of the organ, which makes it a rather ghoulish sight. I pay close attention to the big artery that is rimmed with ugly plaque. I suppose the point of the model is to make you revolt at the sight of a diseased vessel. In this the model is quite successful.

But I wonder, as someone writing a book on the soul of medicine, if there might be a better object of contemplation. What if there were a lovely Quan Yin, the Chinese feminine Buddha of healing and compassion, standing gracefully there on the shelf? I could contemplate the power of life to heal, and I could become more relaxed and optimistic. What if there were a decent painting of Jesus healing a blind person? What if there were music playing, perhaps a song of healing sung by a Native American medicine man? What if there were at least a photograph of a living human being in an ordinary setting having a good time with others? Any of these would be preferable to a sickly plastic model of a diseased, objectified, and detached organ.

Our problem is that we don't understand images. We just see the plastic heart as instructional. We fail to realize that it also serves as an image that penetrates deep into the imagination of the patient, who can't help meditating on it, since it's the focal point of the room. The only other alternatives are the sink and the latex gloves, and one can only imagine where they would take you in fantasy.

The myth that we live by, modernism, has given us immeasurable blessings, but it has also created a serious blind spot. The arts have almost no place in our world. They are either entertainment or investment. Their power to waken the soul and deepen communal life goes unnoticed in a society of facts, information, instruction, and the material manipulation of the world.

We look intelligently at the architecture of a hospital and see flow and efficiency and usable space. We fail to see the imagistic power of that same architecture. We go into a room dominated by a massive imaging machine and we admire the usefulness of the machine for treatment, but we don't notice how Frankensteinian the room appears to a hapless patient subjected to it.

When Mark McKinney, Sharon O'Brien, and I visited Griffin Hospital in Connecticut, the Planetree hospital, the institution that came closest to my own ideal, we were shown an imaging room. The machine itself was hidden in the wall and its façade painted to be color-coordinated with the beautiful, soft hues and textures of the walls and furniture. Sharon commented that you'd think you were walking into a warm room for a social gathering. The technician told us that it cost nothing extra to have the machine painted in the factory to match their decorating needs. For many of these crucial issues of soul, you don't need money as much as you need an imagination that includes the human dimension.

Another symbol in medicine widely discussed today is the white coat doctors wear and the white uniforms nurses still use, in America at least. Medical historians say that the white coat is rather recent, just over one hundred years old. Previously, doctors wore black, perhaps to represent the seriousness of their occupation. White came in with a concern for bacteria and cleanliness. Today some want to get rid of the white coat but there is also a wish among many to be less separate from their patients. They speak of "white coat syndrome": patients' blood pressure readings high because of the presence of the white-coated doctor.[16]

The other object we've already noted is the stethoscope, invented for the practical purpose of listening to movements of the heart, blood, breath, and other elements. It has become a strong symbol of the profession. The stethoscope as symbolic talisman is nothing new but comes from a long imaginative tradition. Worn around the neck, it hearkens back to shamanic healers who also wore a special coat and a solar disk suspended on a leather strap as a chief sign of their work and their status in the community.[17] Like many ritual objects, the stethoscope is a modern vestigial form of an ancient idea: the healer needs power objects on his person as he goes about the demanding task of healing mysterious illnesses.

Medicine men and women in traditional societies understand the importance of symbolic power. A Native American medical shaman may be brilliantly outfitted with feathers and markings and bangles. A Siberian shaman dresses brightly and carries his highly adorned drum and loud shells. Power objects can help a modern doctor bring the deep, archetypal experience of healing into play with a patient. But power objects can be misused and abused. They should help a doctor obtain the power he needs to do his work rather than give him personal power over his patients. I wouldn't recommend losing any such symbolic object in the practice of medicine, but it is sometimes necessary to remind professionals not to use their power for personal gain.

Those concerns aside, a doctor or nurse needs the help that symbolic objects can give. I noticed in my visits to hospitals and medical schools in several countries that most doctors wear ties, even at a time when more casual wear is the norm. I find myself bringing more ties along on my travels. I feel, rightly or wrongly, that I might be dismissed if I am more casual than the doctors I'm talking to. So, even though a tie is not specific to a doctor, he may wear it to maintain his symbolic power base. As long as he doesn't take the power to himself and abuse it, the tie is one more small help in the challenging practice of medicine.

The Patient's Imagery

A patient, on the other hand, is at a disadvantage with his skimpy hospital gown, open at the back and tied with frayed and ineffective strings. Of course, they are made that way for convenience, but they also have symbolic meaning. In the name of practitioner's convenience, millions of people have been embarrassed to be in the hospital because of the undignified and unattractive gowns forced on them. Don't intelligent, educated medical people know that concern about shame, modesty, and dignity doesn't disappear in illness? The highly dressed and power-endowed professionals only increase their superiority with such indignities that they explain away with practicality.

Liza Coleman, who co-founded a company, Medgowns, that created a new style of hospital gown called "Dreamie," understands the power issue, saying that the new, more modest and dignified gown she has designed offers a small measure of control in a situation where patients often feel like they're no longer in charge. Coleman's gowns are made of pure cotton, provide more coverage in the back, and are designed with long-term patients in mind.[18]

In illness, small things matter a great deal, because life has been reduced to the details that would otherwise be overlooked. The world appears again in all its specific ordinariness, and little things mean everything, including the gown you're wearing and what people see when they look at you.

I'm reminded of the day I spoke at Saint Francis Hospital to women dealing with cancer. My co-presenter was Les Gallo-Silver, who told the women exactly what skin care oils to use under certain conditions, how to deal with hair and shampoo and wigs, and how to care for their skin during a long stay in a hospital. I didn't know the importance of these things myself until I looked into the eyes of these women, taking in every bit of advice and obviously profoundly appreciative of this man's expertise. What is the meaning of life? Sometimes it's a hospital gown that covers your butt or a bit of makeup that makes you look almost normal.

Everything, in the end, has strong symbolic potential and touches the imagination, in spite of the always looming presence of the practical. When my daughter was nine or ten, she was swimming in a pool and came up from underwater to hit her head hard on the granite edge of the pool. A friend rushed us to the hospital, where she had a CT scan that cleared her of serious injury. Even today, seven years later, if you ask her about that experience, her eyes will grow wide and she will describe the horror of being shuttled into the giant donut of a machine, as though she were poking at the entrance of hell.

Just lying in a hospital bed is as much a symbolic act as a practical one. You lie there supine, looking up at anyone who appears. You may be confined to your bed or your room or at least the hospital. You see people come and go. You wonder about their lives. They go out into the world and come back to your microcosm of a hospital room. You have a story about your situation. You are in a cave or a prison as well as a healing environment. Often the fantasy experience has more shadow in it than the literal situation.

People are not so rational, especially when they are sick and especially when they are cut off from their ordinary lives. Health-care workers, on the other hand, are very rational. They are proud of their methods, the rigor of their education and research, and their strong hold on what they consider reality, which doesn't give much credence to imagery. So in this regard there can be a significant gap between the professional and the patient.

It would help if medical people could stretch the borders of their education and therefore their thinking. An education in liberal arts, fine arts, literature, and depth psychology would help. There you would learn to appreciate the narratives that patients are living while lying in their beds and the images that stir them, for good or ill, during their treatment.

If research, logic, quantifications, and evidence-seeking are the language of modern social sciences, then imagery is the language of the soul. It is how we dream at night and fantasize during the day, how we write poetry and sing songs, and how we express deep thought and emotion. Imagery arises within us before rational, ordering thought takes over. It arrives drenched in mystery and emotion. It has not yet been dried out through clear thinking. It is closer to our primal wishes and fears than our thoughts are, and so it is both more revealing and more powerful.

It would be useful to the health-care worker to know these things about imagery, because she has to deal with it every day. It lies hidden in every patient's question and statement and behind every machine, room, and procedure of the health-care industry. Place a long, narrow object on a table near a patient and he may quickly develop fantasies about being probed and penetrated. Call it phallic, if you want. Different patients might imagine it differently. Medicine disregards this sort of thing because its attention is elsewhere, in the literal and practical aspects of its instruments and procedures.

The Role of Dreams

All of this imagery hidden in the practical details of medical care comes to a head in the night dreams of the patient, and perhaps of the doctor and nurse. At night our rational thought gives way to the obscure imagery that underlies it during the day. Dream is always ready to break out in the most rational, pragmatic moments. Just begin to get sleepy and discover how the clear thoughts of waking break up into mystifying amalgams of the possible and the improbable. Then consider that those images are laden with much more emotion and significance than thoughts that make sense.

The dream life of patients is at least as worthy of our attention as their waking observations. I have long advocated a second chart to hang on the bed of a patient. The first would keep a record of things like temperature and medications, while the second would be a chart of dreams. What a patient dreams during his illness is like a counterpoint to what he suffers physically. In those dreams are hints about his state of health, his emotions, the meaning of his illness, and its connection to the rest of his life. These details could be of immense value to some visionary thoughtful enough to want to heal the whole person, dreams and all.

Many ancient traditions connect dreams with health and healing. We have already seen how the great healing god of the Greeks, Asklepios, was to be found in his temple of dreams. People with serious sickness would make a pilgrimage to one of his popular temples, offer a sacrifice, and spend the night or more waiting for a dream that would either heal them physically or heal their relationship with their illness.

The ritual of sleeping in the god's temple and waiting for a healing dream was called incubation, and in a sense, as I noted in Chapter 2, a modern-day patient spending days or weeks at a hospital—or just overnight, for that matter—is also incubating. He is incubating his illness, giving it time to reveal itself and, one hopes, heal.

When you incubate, you give yourself time to lie peacefully, waiting, allowing your imagination to come to life and your emotions to stir. Like a bird sitting on an egg, you are doing something essential, even if it looks as though you're doing nothing.

But the incubation of an illness is not all peace and quiet. You may be visited by fears and bad habits of thought. Åke Hultkrantz, professor of comparative religion, who studied North American medicine men and women, tells an interesting story about a man who wanted to become a healing shaman.[19] Shamans-to-be might go on a vision quest or have a night dream or simply find themselves in a dreamlike state in which they were offered the power to heal. One such aspirant, Taivotsi, went on a quest. Years before, he had been told in a dream to go to a certain place, bathe in the creek, and spend the night waiting for a vision. An owl, a bear, a deer, and a coyote came near him, but he wasn't frightened and held his ground. Only when a rattlesnake appeared did he run away. Years later his grandson, telling the story, said that if he could have withstood the snake, he would have become a healer.

Stories like this are mysterious and in many ways seem foreign; nevertheless, they may have something to teach us about being in a hospital or waiting for an X-ray or sitting in an examination room waiting for the doctor to show up. In these moments of incubation, when we are lulled by waiting into a dreamlike state, our fears and anxieties may visit us. The tale of Taivotsi suggests that we have to be strong and patient. It is not only the doctor who may appear to save us, but also a spirit of healing we may sense within us. We have to endure one temptation after another to succumb to the power of the illness. This particular illness may be our rattle-snake, and we have to be ready to face it.

In another context, we'll discuss power and the sado-masochistic aspects of medicine. Here, the issue is the struggle to evoke the healing from within, to avoid collapsing in fear at some perceived threat. The traditional medicine man or woman is someone of profound strength. He is not easily intimidated by the processes of illness and healing.

So, what can an ordinary patient in a hospital learn from an American Plains medicine man? The importance of waiting in stillness for signs of healing. He can prepare himself by cleansing his ideas and behavior so as to bring a certain purity of intention to his healing process. He can be strong, dealing with temptations to succumb and give up. He can look for signs of a real healer—in a doctor, a nurse, or someone else around him.

This Egg Is Not an Egg

René Magritte is famous for his painting of a pipe, entirely realistic and beautiful. Written on the canvas is the message: "*Ceci n'est pas une pipe*" (This is not a pipe). Asked about it, he said, "You can't smoke it." What's the lesson from this surrealist artist? An image is not identical with the thing it represents. I learned this lesson once with my mother.

When my mother was in her final months of life, confined to a room in a convalescent center connected to a hospital, one day she asked for a fresh egg. I was surprised to hear this request, because she wasn't a big egg eater, and I don't remember her ever talking about fresh eggs—except when we were on the farm in New York where her mother grew up and where her grandparents settled after emigrating from Ireland. I thought that maybe her sickness was taking her back to those years. When my wife and I actually brought her a fresh egg, she wasn't interested in it. We were being literal about her waking dream.

I remember, too, that her mother, my grandmother, had similar dream experiences when she was in her last months. She told me that she would go to bed and have to walk carefully around nicely trimmed bushes that surrounded the bed. I was sure that those were the bushes in the yard of the little house where she raised six children, housed her sister with her sister's husband and son, and took in a border to help pay the rent. My grandmother was very fond of that house where she spent most of her life and was able to be there in waking dream at the end.

Patients in hospitals are often at the edge of awareness—drugged, sleepy, bored, anxious, impaired, and isolated. It is only natural that subliminal images will start emerging from them. They may not make sense in what they say. They may be unusually close to memory, desire, and deep feeling. It takes a thoughtful, open-minded health-care worker not to just tolerate this spilling of the soul's imagery but to receive it and appreciate it. If body, soul, and spirit are involved in our sickness—and they must be since they are inseparably what makes us human—then we could be aware of our thoughts and daydreams as we wait and sit and lie.

Patients could pay close attention to the dreams and dreamlike images that come to them as they incubate their illness, waiting for a cure. Doctors and nurses and attendants could take patients' night and day dreams seriously enough to see their importance to the dreamer and resist dismissing them in a modernist distaste for imagery and memory. These are expressions of the soul and have a place in the origins and healing of the illness being treated.

CHAPTER 8

THE SOUL
OF A HOSPITAL

Saint Francis Hospital in Hartford was founded by a small group of Sisters of Saint Joseph who arrived in 1897 from France. The head of the group, Mother Valencia, was a woman obviously dedicated to the work of her faith and, according to all accounts, had a big heart and fearless spine. How this group, none of them medically trained, with no English to speak of, managed to create an enduring health center from an initial cash holding of $9.65 (according to the biography of the founders written by the Jesuit John Louis Bonn[20]) is one of the mysteries of Catholic creativity in America.

Now, over a hundred years later, many citizens of Hartford say that there is something special about Saint Francis Hospital. They compare it to "secular" hospitals in the area and insist that Saint Francis has an atmosphere that must be connected to its Catholic founding.

You don't see many Catholic sisters in the hospital today. Like schools and colleges, hospitals no longer have the benefit of committed "religious" sisters, simply because their numbers are decreasing severely. At Saint Francis I frequently run into Sister Judy Carey, who in one intelligent, friendly, and determined character embodies an entire community of sisters. As I already explained in relation to the mission statement, Sister Judy uses all of her powers of persuasion and influence to have the hospital's idealistic mission carried out by every member of the staff.

But I don't think Sister Judy or CEO Christopher Dadlez's focus on the mission of the hospital explains its special atmosphere. Perhaps it's the phenomenon you see in many institutions: origins often determine character, unless there is a marked departure from original values, as when a large corporation takes over a smaller business. Saint Francis came into being step by step through spiritual values rather than matters of profit or even simple medical ambition. The originating sisters were not educated in medicine, not even nursing, and yet they brought a strong and lasting vision to this particular place, and somehow that vision endures.

I suppose I could use one of my favorite words at this point: *myth*. As a theologian and religion specialist, I use the word in a specific sense, not to mean falsehood or empty fantasy, but rather the narrative, largely unconscious, that underlies and powers a society or a community. I use *myth* the way Joseph Campbell popularized it. He listed four ways in which a myth informs a community:

1. To connect to the mysteries inherent in the world we inhabit—the mystical function.

2. To create a meaningful understanding of the natural world—the cosmological function.

3. To establish and maintain values and an ethical way of life—the moral function.

4. To allow the individual to develop into a person who belongs to and can thrive in the world and the community—the psychological function.

These functions of myth apply in particular ways to a hospital, just as they would to any other community. The first one, the notion of mystery, may be the most important one of all in setting a spiritually attuned hospital apart from others. At Saint Francis you will find a chapel, a mosque, and an active and influential program of pastoral care. But beyond what is visible, you sense a deep assumption among staff and benefactors that health care is not only a right for everyone but the spiritual duty of all men and women, whether or not they are in the field of medicine. This hospital doesn't turn patients away, and its budget suffers accordingly.

I have seen the values of the founders, not just the mission statement, carried on in many staff members and benefactors. They don't make a big issue of it; they simply embody those values. Many say that they were drawn to Saint Francis because of its spiritual atmosphere and its values, and maybe that is how the spirit continues.

My friend Mark McKinney is a good example. He attended Andover Newton Theological School, where he studied Jungian psychology. He also graduated from a Baptist seminary. Mark knows hospital life very well, being deep on the inside for over 20 years. He also has a big heart and embraces community in every way. He has created imaginative programs teaching pastoral counselors, helping obese people lose weight through community offerings, and arranging for gang members to work for the hospital, especially where their gangmates are being treated.

Mark has an interesting presence in the hospital. His job description ranges far and wide. He is not a typical representative of a particular belief system but understands the richness and breadth of the spiritual life. His knowledge of psychology is deep and sophisticated. In short, he is a treasure to his hospital and to his state, which uses his expertise and imagination in a variety of ways.

Having one person like Mark on staff helps spread soul all around the place. His sheer presence keeps these values in mind, and his participation in meetings and the programs he creates speak for the soul, when otherwise purely practical wisdom would prevail. Mark is not a New Age sentimentalist; his intelligence gives his alternative philosophy substance and weight in an environment where education and sophistication count considerably.

Fortunately, many medical centers have a similar person or persons who keep soul and spirit in the forefront through their presence. I have watched Dr. Mary Jo Kreitzer at the University of Minnesota, Dr. Balfour Mount at McGill University, and Rev. George Doebler at the University of Tennessee carry this awareness in their persons as they offer daily inspiration and guidance to very large institutions. They not only do extraordinary work, they embody a vision that is like a potent seed offering our medical institutions a real future.

You could say that at one level the soul of a hospital is its people, especially those people who consistently bring soul values to their daily work. A soulful hospital doesn't appear from nowhere. It takes the constant, imaginative presence of people of heart and vision speaking up, working in their special way, and advocating an alternative myth for contemporary medicine.

A Natural, Healing Place

Every time I consider what goes into making a soulful hospital, I go back to two basic elements: nature and architecture. Marsilio Ficino said that from the point of view of soul architecture is the most important of the arts. It makes sense that a soulful building will constantly remind you and urge you to work in a certain reflective and caring way. A purely functional kind of architecture will turn you into a machine.

Vincent Scully makes a similar point in his book on Greek temples.[21] They comprise, he says, two levels: the natural setting, which itself embodies the spirit to be worshipped and honored, and the temple architecture, which is the embodiment of the god or goddess's particular qualities. About the temple of Asklepios specifically he says, "Most of his sites are calm and enclosed, medically salubrious, psychologically relaxing." A good suggestion for the building and décor of our hospitals.

Today most hospitals seems to have given up the ancient idea, going all the way back to the early Greeks, that a place of healing ought to be in an especially impressive natural setting and that it should be a temple to the spirits of health (Hygeia) and medicine (Asklepios). Our hospitals often convey just the opposite. They are factory-like boxes of machinery. Scully mentions a small temple to Aphrodite at one of the Asklepian sites and notes that she is "essential to healing." That is to say that beauty and sensuality have an important role in healing.

Today many hospitals have quiet rooms for meditation, and these rooms are focal points for the spirit and soul in healing, creating sanctuaries to counter the sprawling buildings and long, crisscrossing hallways. In some places, though, these empty rooms are plain empty and don't evoke the spirit of contemplation and transcendence. It isn't easy to get it right: create a spiritual space in which people from many traditions will feel comfortable and at home. My preference is for multidenominational representation rather than nondenominational. I would like to see healer santos and Jesus and Buddha and Quan Yin rather than sheer emptiness.

Spirituality is largely about the presence of God or the presence of mystery or the presence of holy beings—angels, bodhisattvas, dakini, or holy men and women who model or convey the spirit. Spirituality need not be abstract. It can have its own soul through images, color, and sacred and beautiful objects.

Religion specialists have a word for the power of a spiritual presence—*numinosity*. The word comes from the Latin *numen*, "having a strong spiritual quality or suggesting the presence of a divinity." A place can be numinous. You feel the power and presence, as when you enter a Gothic cathedral and feel your breath expand. The numinous is similar to awe. It would be a good thing for hospitals to be built and arranged in such a way that the awesome potency of healing permeates the place, affecting all who enter it and who stay there and work there.

Listen to the 2nd-century traveler and guide Pausanias as he describes the great sanctuary of Asklepios in Epidauros:

> The sacred grove of Asklepios has boundary-stones around it in every direction. Inside that enclosure, no men die and no women bear children. Everyone consumes his sacrifice inside the boundaries. The statue of Asklepios is made of ivory and gold. He sits enthroned holding a staff, with one hand over the serpent's head, and a dog lying beside him. Over from the temple is where the ritual suppliants of the god go to sleep. A round construction of white stone called Round House has been built nearby. Inside is a picture by Pausias in which Eros has discarded his bow and arrows, and carries a lyre instead. In my day there are six left of the stone tablets standing in the enclosure, though there were more in antiquity. The names of men and women healed by Asklepios are engraved on them, with the diseases and how they were healed.[22]

I quote this passage because it provides a fascinating description of a healing place, when people still honored the sacred nature of medicine. Notice that the sacred space is defined by a grove and stones. There is a hint for how to create a healing environment. The statue of Asklepios is shown with the snake, the staff, and his dog. Today we use the staff and snake as a symbol of medicine but perhaps without the numinosity Pausanias describes. It's also interesting that there was a painting of Eros with a lyre instead of weapons. Maybe in sickness the struggles of love become only memories to recite or sing.

Pausanias refers in passing to a round stone enclosure. This was the tholos, a beautiful building with elaborate classical columns rising 20 feet and a floor of white and black marble. No one is certain what the building was used for. Under the floor is a circular labyrinth in which, some say, the snakes sacred to Asklepios were kept. (A separate building, the abaton, housed the people who came to the sanctuary looking for a cure.) Imagine such a potent sacred space in a contemporary hospital, a space simply for presenting the power of the healing spirit.

The soul of a hospital resides in the awesome spirit of healing found there. That spirit might be reflected in the architecture and décor or in the attitude of those who work there. The day I walked through Griffin Hospital, the Planetree hospital in Connecticut, the doctor from the Netherlands who joined us on the tour kept saying, "My hospital is a factory compared to this." Many hospitals give the impression of being factories for rebuilding bodies rather than temples of health and healing, and that is another way of saying that they lack soul.

The Hospital as a Community

People often think of the soul as something an individual person has. But soul is not easily kept within the boundaries of a person. It spreads over into family, friends, lovers, and ultimately community. After studying many traditional descriptions of soul, I picture it as a series of concentric circles, starting with the very deepest point in ourselves, extending through our close relationships, then to our local and national communities, and finally to the earth and beyond. All of these dimensions connect at the level of soul. With the idea that the soul makes an axe an axe, the soul of my country makes me an American, of my religion a Catholic, of my deepest mind and heart a mysterious individual that even I can't define.

The soul of a hospital is also to be found in the people who make it all work and come to it for help and support it. The whole health-care community joined with patients and their families. Do these people feel connected? Are the workers engaged in the calling or just doing a job? Do they treat each other as individuals? Do they care about their work and the people around them? Do they find meaning beyond their immediate practical concerns; that is, do they see a spiritual dimension to their work? When these conditions are present, the soul comes into view and transforms the place from a factory into a place of healing, into the grove of Asklepios.

A community is not a mere collection of people. A community is largely an invisible element that you may or may not sense in a group. It is the bond, the connection, the eros rather than the sheer quantity. Eros is a form of love in which the accent is on desire and pleasure. Eros is not sentimental or romantic but the magnetism that draws people to each other and to their work. It's a love that needs awareness, reflection, and attention. It doesn't happen automatically. People need to talk to each other, have some downtime to connect, and perhaps eat informally together.

Two problems in particular make community difficult to sustain. One is the mistaken notion that community is a collection of like-minded people. No, a real community

is a gathering of individuals, people who think for themselves and can express their viewpoints. The other problem
is narcissism—individuals who doubt their worth and their
substance. They feel a need to be somebody special, because
they don't sense their individual gifts. Narcissism pushes
a person away from community toward self-need. It isn't
a moral problem, as it is often seen, but a psychological
one. Narcissistic people simply need the opportunity to be
recognized honestly for what they do. They need expressed
appreciation and acceptance. Without it, they force attention on themselves and find community feeling a threat to
their standing.

Hospitals are stratified organizations, with many levels
and hierarchies. In some places these levels work as a caste
system, with clear indications of position and status. Many
have a number of separate buildings, and one specialty
might feel exiled in a remote place. One group in a hospital may not know anything about the personnel or job
descriptions of another. Sections don't communicate with
each other. Stratification can lead to suspicion and para-
noia, certainly a lot of gossip. Maybe this is just community with its shadow components, but in many instances
there is no doubt that it would help to change chaos into
community.

One day a receptionist in the emergency room talked
about her work with considerable pride. She understood
that she was in the position of first contact with patients,
and that made her job crucial. She knew that she was part
of a community, and she felt appreciated.

At Saint Francis I walked around the intensive-care unit
with a heart surgeon who knew everyone we encountered
and called them by name. He had a friendly manner and a
refreshing humility about his role. I thought that this man
had the qualities needed to sustain the hospital community
from his end quite effectively, and I thought that for the
soul of the hospital he was indispensable.

As a guest speaker in many hospital settings, I've had the opportunity to meet sponsors, contributors, and trustees, whose main job is to keep the hospital solvent. Generally, these people, too, reflect the soul of the place. They will be cool about the values of the hospital or, more likely, deep in the spirit of the place and eager to tout its virtues and strengths. I wonder sometimes if they know how important their role is in sustaining not only the physical well-being of the institution but its spirit and soul as well.

The Healing Powers of the Soul

A few years ago I was feeding my two dogs, one an aged collie and the other a young and energetic mutt. I had a bowl of dog food in each hand, and when I tried to walk into the house from the porch I tripped over a door-mat and fell, hitting my forehead hard on the sharp edge of the doorjamb. I was alone in the house and was dazed at first. When I came to, I saw blood all over my hands and felt a lump on my bleeding head. I sat down, not knowing what to do, since I couldn't think clearly. At that moment my wife and daughter arrived from a shopping trip and drove me immediately to the emergency room of our local hospital. I walked into a crowded reception area and was told to wait my turn and get my insurance information out. I couldn't think very clearly, but I had enough presence of mind to see that this visit would be good material for my book.

My first impression was not a positive one. The receptionists were too busy and rushed. Maybe they did a quick triage and decided I had minor abrasions. There were people present with serious problems. But I was treated brusquely and felt no sense of care. I didn't feel that I was in a place of healing as much as a "factory" where the assembly line was moving too quickly.

Eventually a harried doctor came and gave me a dozen stitches. He didn't introduce himself and I didn't think he went about his work with a great deal of care. The scar on my forehead even today is very noticeable, while the work the plastic surgeon did on my face when he removed my precancerous lesion is impossible to detect. Maybe it was just a matter of skill—a plastic surgeon versus an emergency room resident. I suspect that the lack of soul in that place was also a factor, because ultimately it is the soul that heals, even when it is only a matter of stitches.

The soul is the invisible factor that draws people together, brings out their humanity, and gives depth and meaning to whatever they do. When you treat people as objects, as cases and syndromes and machines in need of repair, you will not be a healer, not even a doctor or nurse. You will be a technician, a human repairman, a functionary in a world of objects. Soul will not enter into your work, not into your skillful use of techniques and not into your relationship with your patients. Your work will not satisfy you, not because it isn't worthy work but because there is no soul to give it a deep human pulse.

On the other hand, when soul is present, when you are capable of being present as a human being and making a connection to a patient, even simple applications of your skills will make your work fulfilling and bring you close in touch with the people who come to you for help.

A hospital with soul is a place of healing. A hospital without soul is a body repair shop. The depth of human feeling and care will show itself in the people, in the building and in the atmosphere. In a sense, it is the atmosphere that heals. Religion scholar Karoly Kerenyi once wrote that you sense the presence of the god in the atmosphere of a place. In a hospital you may sense the presence of Asklepios. If you do, whether or not you name him, you will know that the place has soul and that it has what is required to heal.

PART III

HEALING WITH GRACE

*At peace above my sickness
summer smolders.*

— HAKUSETSU

CHAPTER 9

SERVICE TO HUMANITY

I have already referred to Albert Schweitzer's three-word statement that guided all of his work: reverence for life. I would like to offer another three-word philosophy that could lie at the base of medical practice: service to humanity.

Most doctors and nurses say that they would do the work even if they weren't paid for it. They are indeed concerned, as they should be, to be paid a good wage for their work. They mean, rather, that their job in medicine represents their desire to be of service to humanity. When you ask people in the medical professions what brought them to the work, they will often say, "I wanted to help people."

It's a basic, perhaps obvious idea: Medical people want to be of service. That desire is at the very root of their existence and their getting up to go to work every day. But almost everyone in medicine I interviewed said that today it isn't easy to live by such a simple principle. The complexities of medical education, insurance, and malpractice pressures get in the way.

When a professional is dedicated to giving service, he knows what work has to be done, but today many feel that the bureaucracy makes this kind of service difficult. You have to compromise with requirements, and you have to arrange your work so that you are paid enough to cover the steep prices of malpractice insurance, office space, and other professional expenses.

At one level, then, the doctor or other professional has to deal with the endless demands on time and money, and at another level he has to try to keep the soul in the work. Many, of course, just succumb to necessity and forget about their ideals and their calling. Others feel burned out by the process and look for a way out.

An Expanded Medical Vision

Books on the history of medicine are often dismissive of the past. They present Western medicine as an evolution toward science and machinery and celebrate each advance over what they judge to be ignorance. The history books rarely take a lesson from the past or challenge modern approaches by comparing them to past methods. They can't see beyond technical backwardness to the philosophical and spiritual riches in medicine of the pre-technological age.

It is possible to read old medical books with an eye toward their wisdom. Of course, we have made a multitude of dazzling discoveries in recent decades, but we haven't advanced the philosophical and spiritual aspects very far. In this, the ancients are still ahead of us.

A good example is the writing of Paracelsus, whose work with alchemy and astrology would cause eyes to roll today. His philosophy of medicine is inspiring and rich and could well address some of the emotional and spiritual issues that are problematic in contemporary medical practice.

Consider the following passage, which I have reflected on for years: "In medicine we should never lose heart, and never despair. For each ill there is a remedy that combats it. Thus there is no disease that is inevitably mortal. All diseases can be cured, without exception. Only because we do not know how to deal with them properly, because we are unable to understand life and death in their essence, can we not defend ourselves against them."[23] Paracelsus was born in 1493.

Cross-cultural studies in medicine also offer new, creative ideas that could complement and enrich modern medical practice. Traditional healing methods are quite different from Western approaches, yet they, too, usually work from a larger picture of what a human being is. Shamanic healers, for example, take into account both psychological and spiritual aspects of a person's experience and respond to them accordingly, with rituals and potent images.

A modern doctor could study a shaman's way of healing and deepen his own practice without literally adopting shamanic techniques, or he could become shamanic in his own way. He could learn to meditate in such a way that he discovered a layered universe and could get to know realms of imagination that might enrich his practice. We live in one world, where it is possible to combine universes of meaning and method.

A doctor might learn from a shaman how to evoke levels of awareness through music or other types of sound. He could learn to stop and look at images in his dreams and waking fantasy life that otherwise he would pass by. He could learn that to be a real healer you discover how to be a conduit of healing power. All of this could be adopted in a subtle way within modern practice.

Many years ago I did a preliminary study, a sort of test case, on asthma. I looked into the history of the word and the way the illness has been treated over the centuries. I was looking for insights into the soul and spirit of the disease. I found that the word *asthma* is related to the word *aesthetics*, both having to do with taking the world in. I found the word used in ancient Greek literature for the last dying gasp of warriors and later as a suffocating feeling from being dominated by another person. Psychoanalytic literature placed asthma in the context of maternal pressures. I read a biography of the French writer Marcel Proust, who said that his writing emerged in part from his asthma, in particular to his extreme sensitivity to the world around him.

None of these ideas offered a "cure" for the disease, and my approach certainly moved in a direction far different from clinical studies of asthma, but this kind of research did address the human dimension of the experience of asthma. I believe it did offer insight that could, if developed and extended, help deal with the disease in a holistic manner.

I am speaking here of the "humanity" part of the life philosophy "service to humanity." We doctors, nurses, and therapists want to help people—the accent on people, not just bodies. We want to help people go through their illnesses and live happy and creative lives. I would like to help people deepen as persons because of their illness, treating it as a rite of passage rather than the mere failure of a physical system. But it isn't easy to advocate a holistic viewpoint when the spirit of the times moves strongly in a different direction, toward specialization, literalism, and the enthronement of science.

Today you see this last idea in a catchword common in medicine—*evidence.* Researchers and practitioners are proud of what they call evidence-based medicine. The gist of this approach is to select treatment for a given patient based on reliable studies that have been carried out on various possible treatments and issues related to the problem, linked to the clinician's decision-making in the face of a patient's situation. Using this approach, health-care professionals make "conscientious, explicit, and judicious use of current best evidence" in making decisions about the care of the individual patient. It means "integrating individual clinical expertise with the best available external clinical evidence from systematic research."[24]

Guidelines for this approach rank various kinds of research studies for their appropriateness as standards of evidence. They also suggest that the clinician should not lose sight of his or her own experience but should nevertheless put more weight by far on evidential studies. Furthermore, this approach works on two levels: in an organization, such as a hospital or clinic that evaluates its effectiveness based on evidential studies, and with the individual caregiver, who conscientiously researches the evidence when making a choice about treatment.

You can see the value of consulting studies about treating medical issues that have been dealt with thousands of times. The physician or nurse doesn't have to invent the wheel every time he or she faces a knotty medical problem. On the other hand, many worry about this approach, fearing that it will override a physician's medical experience and intuition, cause insurance companies to approve only those protocols supported by evidence, and disregard important issues in illness and treatment that are not covered by evidence.

My concern is that evidence-based medicine may become yet another form of impersonal, science-dominated health care. It's a kind of standardization of care that looks reasonable on the surface but could create even more distance between the practitioner and the patient. Where is the soul in evidence-based medicine?

The Meaning of Service

Taking "service to humanity" as our mantra, exactly how do we offer service when we're getting paid? How do we see our work as service when we are applying ideas and techniques that we have learned through study and practice in higher education? Can we really be offering service when we're doing our jobs rather than volunteering?

Service is related to the words *servant* and *servile,* all of which go back to the Latin word, *servus,* for slave. Service is not slavery, but it does have the connotation of emptying oneself for the benefit of another. Preparing for this book, I talked to a great number of people in the health services, people in every imaginable job related to medicine and in many different institutions and countries. Most of them understood that their calling was to serve, and they found rewards in doing so.

The service aspect might appear in their attitude toward their work and toward their patients. They felt that they were serving when they went even a short distance past what was required of them: spending more time at work on behalf of a patient, spending more time in the patient's presence, being more available by talking freely or sitting rather than standing. That is an interesting notion—service through sitting with a patient, showing her that you are not ready to run off to the next chore or assignment.

The key of service in these examples is going slightly beyond the requirements of the job on behalf of a patient. Dr. Baxter's stories of his AIDS patients in New York show that service is not only an offering of time, but also personal, emotional effort to do what is necessary for the complete healing of the patient. Dr. Baxter worked for the entire welfare of his patients, attending them not only so that they would have the best medical treatment available but also that they might have a meaningful death. He gave his attention to their families and to the aftermath of the suffering and death of a loved one. He had his limits, of course, but they extended beyond what most would consider his duties as a physician.

Albert Schweitzer not only practiced medicine, he moved to a poor area of Africa and treated needy patients.

My plastic surgeon not only did excellent work for his pay-ing patients at home, he traveled to remote areas to offer his skills to children with cleft palates, places where, with-out his intervention, they would suffer their scars for their entire lives. My friend Mark McKinney goes out of his way to embrace the people of his city, including gang members, who might otherwise lie outside the sphere of concern of a busy hospital. At the University of Tennessee, George Doebler picks up all the pieces of humanity in need, wher-ever he sees them. Dr. Balfour Mount goes far beyond the expertise of his medical training to create inventive pro-grams for the souls of the citizens of Montreal. The list of medical professionals who indeed feel a calling to service and accomplish it by extending the limits of their creative work is endless. Here we see the soul of medicine: a deep feeling for humanity showing itself in many compassionate and creative modes of service.

There is also a psychological side to service. When you truly serve people, instead of merely doing a job for them, you connect with them. You meet them at a common level or point of interest. One of the chief psychological blocks to service on the part of doctors is the arrogance patients run up against time after time. Arrogance lies at the oppo-site end of the spectrum from an attitude of service, so one wonders if arrogance in the medical profession is an active avoidance of service.

One form of arrogance is the doctor who doesn't want you, the patient, to think for yourself or do any study of your problem or go beyond the boundaries of strict Western medical science. A renowned doctor who writes in a major magazine warned people against scouring the Internet for information on their diseases. The best patients, he said, are those who do as he says and come to him as the expert.

A savvy public health official told me that, in contrast, young doctors, raised on video games and skilled at com-puters, welcome patients who educate themselves on their diseases and treatments. There is a significant generational gap, she said, that separates the hot young democratic doctors from the remote, autocratic old physicians who want their patients to obey them to the letter.

People who are used to going online for most of their needs would find it natural to study their illness in that way. I suspect that it's a neurotic need for authority and control that keeps some doctors from joining their patients in studying their medical issues online.

Another form of arrogant healer is the doctor who is too busy to bother answering naïve questions or getting involved with the families of patients, who are always asking about something. This is a kind of class arrogance, a professional who won't stoop to the level of lay ignorance that his patients and their families, in his mind, display.

Some forms of arrogance you can see in dress and comportment, the "bedside manner" of the doctor. Even friendly, laughing, joking doctors can be arrogant in their low esteem of anyone not in their profession.

One day I sat with a group of nurses in the birthing unit of an East Coast hospital. They loved their work so much that they said that if they went a short while without attending a birth, they felt empty and yearned to get back to duty. They e-mailed and phoned from home to see how their patients were doing. Their involvement, they said, was 24/7.

And yet their devotion to their chosen work was overshadowed by an insensitive hospital hierarchy that expected more from them than they could deliver and refused to give them the space and personnel they needed. I could feel both the strength of their dedication and the depth of their disgust with the top-heavy hierarchy that didn't yet understand the professional status of the ob-gyn nurse.

Studies on doctor arrogance raise some interesting points: Doctors are often unconscious of their arrogance. They may not recognize it until a patient's lawyer points it out to them. Doctors excuse arrogance, blaming it on a tough training program and the impossible job of treating people in life-and-death situations. Some doctors confuse arrogance with courage and risk-taking, positive and needed attitudes in a field full of new adventures and experiments.

One of the best explanations for professional arrogance I have found is one offered by the Swiss Jungian analyst Adolf Guggenbühl-Craig. He talks about a split archetype, a problem we have already noted. In the best of situations, a doctor treats a patient as a fellow human being, both of them susceptible to mistakes and illness, both having intelligence and good intuitions. But usually this archetype of healing, which has two sides—healer and patient—gets literalized and split up between the two people. The doctor is the healer and the patient the one to be healed. The doctor forgets that he is human, too, and is sometimes a patient. The patient forgets, or may not even realize, that she plays a positive role in the healing and can make good judgments and have helpful intuitions as well. This is fertile ground for the dangerous and disrupting condition of doctor arrogance.

Guggenbühl-Craig describes the situation perfectly. "The doctor is no longer able to see his own wounds, his own potential for illness; he sees sickness only in the other. He objectifies illness, distances himself from his own weakness, elevates himself and degrades the patient."[25]

The solution to this split archetype is to face yourself, acknowledge your arrogance, and make a genuine effort to do something about it. Notice your defensiveness when people give you hints about it. Face your anxieties, your attitude toward your work, and your fears.

When I first began practicing psychotherapy, I realized that I wasn't fully prepared for the work. I didn't know some things I should know because I hadn't faced them in my own life. My first years in this work were effective—I had a good education and good training—but they were difficult because of the personal work on my own soul I knew I had to do. I went into therapy myself, I kept a full and intense diary of my inner conflicts and my dreams, and I consulted with many professional and nonprofessional friends. I reached a point where I finally felt more secure in myself as a healer. I saw some good work I had done, but because of my self-confrontations I didn't gloat over it.

This experience of mine leads me to think that self-confrontation is an important step in becoming a healer. Like the aspiring Plains healer who didn't become a shaman because of his fear of rattlesnakes, many physicians fail to evoke the healer in their work because of their fears, and they won't deal with those fears until they face up to them.

A physician doesn't have to be afraid as long as his patient bears all the weight of anxiety around his illness. But in the best situation, the two share their fears and enjoy the genius for healing that they also share. The cure for doctors' arrogance is to appreciate the wisdom and capability that ordinary people bring to their illnesses, and even the insights and deep intelligence in their families. The cure lies in the shared experience of suffering and doctoring, the evocation of healing rather than one person working on another. We are brought back to our mantra, service to humanity. The realization of our common humanity keeps the doctor from being arrogant and the patient from being passive.

Of course, some people live by superstition and unfounded fears and truisms that they have picked up in their families. Some get erroneous information from the Internet. Some have psychological problems that make them poor candidates for sharing healing power with their doctors. But Dr. Baxter's examples show how even the slightest participation in the healing process might be useful.

The psychology of service could be one of those human issues that find their way into the soulful education of a health-care worker. It isn't enough to encourage, inspire, or cajole a person to show some etiquette with patients. Each worker has to do some work on or with himself, dealing with emotional issues that any of us might have that may interfere with good community relationships. The soul exists in the rich, sometimes tense space between people, and how you handle that space can make all the difference in creating a healing environment.

CHAPTER 10

NURSE RATCHED AND THE MARQUIS DE SADE

Many years ago, when I was a novice psychotherapist learning how to deal with violence and aggression in my patients, a respected teacher, Rafael Lopez-Pedraza, suggested that I read the Marquis de Sade for insight. So I bought cheap, thick paperback versions of his books and began reading. I discovered why he is reviled so much—his scenes are revolting for their depictions of violence, sexual perversion, and blasphemy. But I came to believe Sade when he says that he is a novelist with a profound interest in human depravity. He wants to search out its roots and understand it through his fiction. He himself was revolted by the aggression that polite society directs toward its victims under the cloak of social responsibility. I wrote a book, *Dark Eros,* treating Sade as an insightful writer who offers deep insight into evil.

In my book I first made a distinction between Sadean situations and sadomasochistic behavior. Every interaction between people involves some exercise of power and openness. In that sense every interaction involves Sadean power issues. A mother asks a child not to go out to play until she has cleaned up her room. The child feels the pain of not being able to do what her heart desires, perhaps passionately. But she succumbs to her mother's will and straightens her room, putting off her own pleasures. A child may learn much from this interaction, even though it is painful. There is no harm done—no physical or emotional abuse. It is a simple, common interaction that involves pain and learning.

School is another Sadean enterprise. A teacher makes his students study for an exam. They have to put off pleasant plans for parties and outings to do so, and the study may be painful. But they learn, and they are not harmed emotionally or physically by the test. In fact, they may enjoy and appreciate the way their teacher has instructed them.

These examples are ordinary situations where there is real exercise of power and real and painful subjugation. But all the parties agree to the arrangement and recognize that ultimately it benefits the "victims."

The medical world is also rich in Sadean scenarios. Just go to a dentist and look at the long needles he uses and the sharp, curved, pointed instruments. You not only submit to his painful ministrations, you pay him well for them. You want healthy teeth and a nice smile, so you go through the pain willingly, and he is happy to inflict the pain for your benefit. The same is true for many medical treatments. They may be frightening and painful, but you are all too happy to give yourself over to them.

I remember the day in my 20th year when I was playing soccer on a muddy field in Northern Ireland. I was enjoying the game when suddenly I felt a sharp pain in my lower left abdomen. I had to leave the pitch and go to my room in the monastery school where I was living. That evening a local doctor came and drove me to the hospital in Dungannon, a small nearby town. Ordinarily I would hate the thought of being operated on, but the pain was so severe that I couldn't wait to be wheeled into the operating room and get on with it. I was a very willing subject, happy to have my skin lanced and my innards cut out. Today I have happy memories of that whole situation. The appendectomy saved my life, and I've lived well ever since.

The medical world is full of Sadean scenes, where patients are victims of sorts and doctors and others are the "torturers"—all for the benefit of the victims.

But human psychology is balanced on a precariously thin line between necessity and acting out. Sadean situations can easily slip into sadomasochism, which is the splitting of the archetype. When the pattern of inflicting/suffering pain holds together, both sides appreciate what has to be done and participate willingly. But when the archetype pulls apart, one person inflicts pain on the other without agreement and without mutual benefit. One person is the sadist and the other the masochist, one the perpetrator of aggression and the other the victim of it.

When the archetype is intact, both people are happy. When the archetype splits, one person enjoys inflicting pain, and mysteriously the other enjoys being the victim. This was the startling discovery of Leopold von Sacher-Masoch, a novelist and man of letters who described in psychological detail the pleasures some people find in being victimized. Later, Richard von Krafft-Ebing, a student of unusual sexual behavior, coined the word *masochism,* defining it as "the wish to suffer pain and be subjected to force."[26]

Our word *sadomasochism* comes from the work of two novelists who understood that both the infliction of suffering and the feeling of pain and being dominated can be pleasurable and desired. Krafft-Ebing described this broad, complicated process in lurid sexual language, but it also makes sense in an ordinary way of thinking. Anyone might enjoy the experience of having someone else take over and tell him or her what to do. If you go on an adventure in nature, you may be happy to have a guide giving you precise instructions. In a very deep way this willingness may have roots in sexuality, but it also simply makes sense. You can find pleasure in being dominated. I sometimes think about this issue when I'm giving a lecture and I see a hundred or more people in front of me, confined to their seats in a darkened room on a beautiful day. They could be out enjoying themselves, but they choose to be held in check by a lecturer while sitting on uncomfortable chairs. This is not masochism; it's a Sadean arrangement that everyone involved more or less appreciates. But if their boss required them to sit there and suffer, then the situation might turn into sadomasochism.

Probably without realizing it, doctors and nurses sometimes make the slip into sadomachism. They find pleasure in making other people do their will and succumb to their authority. Nurse Ratched, of Ken Kesey's *One Flew over the Cuckoo's Nest*, comes to life as an inspiration for domination, forcing her patients to do her will.

I have always thought it interesting that the Marquis de Sade, who spent much of his life in prison, was moved from prison to a mental institution where he wrote and directed plays for his fellow patients. I see him as a doctor of psychology, and there he is in the late 18th century, doing art therapy in a hospital.

Strong but Gracious

Power and dominance in medical practice bring us back to the theme of arrogance. Patients complain about it worldwide. Arrogance is an aspect of power confusion, and it reflects egomania and extreme anxiety. No one has to control others unless he himself is insecure. Doctors express this insecurity when they defend themselves by saying that they have an impossible job and are not allowed to make mistakes.

Arrogance is a form of neurosis and is therefore a block to soul. It gets in the way of communal exchange and deprives a patient of his or her active role in the community that is health care. Notoriously, arrogant doctors also make the lives and work of nurses difficult. In my visits to medical centers, many nurses told me that, being so close to their patients, they often know more about them than the doctors who won't stoop to take a nurse seriously. There are also many published cases in which a patient has died because a doctor thought it was beneath him or her to listen to a nurse's concerns.

I don't want to speak moralistically about arrogance, suggesting some moral fault in doctors who get carried away with their knowledge and power. It is a psychological issue that comes with the job. As usual, following the mantra from archetypal psychology, I would suggest refining the arrogance into the more substantive quality of which it is only a symptom.

To do a demanding job like doctoring and nursing requires a big person, by which I mean someone who takes life seriously, enjoys his skills, and applies them boldly. If a doctor is arrogant, maybe he needs to grow bigger in the job, even though people around him might wish him to be smaller. Go with the symptom. Take it as a sign of where the soul needs to move. Take bigger risks, go further in the profession, and make as much of the calling as possible. But do it with grace and style. Don't be a small person pretending to be big. Don't abuse the big power and big prestige that goes with the role, but be adequate to it. Be as creative and as skilled as your reputation would have it.

Deep in the American psyche—I don't see it as a character trait in all cultures—is a sentimental valuing of humility, not real humility but an "aw, shucks" attitude that "I'm just doing my job." This false humility is a setup for its opposite, arrogance. Real humility is a precious virtue in anyone, especially a health-care worker. But if humility is false, arrogance is sure to be there hiding in the background. Even if the doctor tries hard to hide it, you sense it, and it makes you immune to the doctor's knowledge and skills.

A person who is neither arrogant nor falsely humble knows and enjoys her power and doesn't have to dominate people to feel strong. She can enjoy her skills and knowledge, but knowing herself well, she also knows her limits and is comfortable with them. An arrogant person has to prop up her reputation by pretending that she has no limitations. That is why I suspect arrogance when doctors make much of the fact that they are not supposed to make mistakes or fail.

My teenage daughter once had a conversation with a psychologist I know. Afterward, she told me that she found him arrogant. I was surprised, not because I didn't know that the man was arrogant, but because I had never heard her use the word before. "I know," I said, "he does very good work but he's unsure of himself. He can't make a mistake or be seen as failing in any way."

"But he's an accomplished person. He's smart. People admire him. Why does he have to be arrogant?"

"Because," I said, trying to explain, "for all his brilliance and achievement, psychologically he's insecure. He can't take the risk of just being himself. He would feel inadequate."

A real failure humbles us and gets us in touch with our humanity. After all, human beings fail. Godlike people don't allow themselves to fail, or at least to be seen to fail. Doctors are under great pressure, both moral and financial, not to fail. Maybe the only way they can remain human is to strive to be as successful as possible in extreme situations and then, in lesser moments, show their weaknesses.

I write at length about arrogance because it is one of the most significant emotional issues in the practice of medicine, one that causes serious problems with patients and co-workers. Yet it only requires some reflection, some open and honest discussion, and some effort to tame arrogance and transform it into greatness of character.

To repeat, I say, "Go with the symptom." If you're arrogant, don't try to be humble. You'll get it all wrong. Turn your arrogance into justified pride and the sheer joy of doing work for your community. You deserve immense gratitude and recognition for what you do. When you receive recognition, accept it and enjoy it fully. This will help you avoid the arrogance that comes from recognition and gratitude denied. But always work hard at deserving the praise you crave.

An arrogant person might also learn how to accept praise and recognition directly and simply, with no neurotic denials or obfuscations. A grateful family member says, "Doctor, you're wonderful." You can say, "Thank you, I love my work and hope to get even better at it."

The Antidote to Big: Big

The solution to big egos among doctors, big salaries that don't satisfy very deeply, and big, puffy programs that don't produce much is not to get small but to get big in a better way. Go with the symptom. Treat the problems of bigness with big ideas and big heart. We see hospitals everywhere expanding and sprawling and towering over cities and neighborhoods, but we don't see the idea of medicine getting equally big. If anything, it is shrinking. It is becoming more controlled by insurance companies, more specialized, reduced to evidence-based treatments, and more tightly limited to the demands of the scientific method and to the modernist philosophy.

I was trying to explain evidence-based medicine to a friend. "You mean," he said, "you get ideas for treatment from all over the world, all systems of healing, and all traditions, and come up with a very rich plan?"

"No," I said. "You take only evidence that has been strictly approved by the scientific research methods and don't allow any personal intuition or any cross-cultural influences. The world doesn't work the way we think it should."

What if we could expand our notions of illness and treatment: learn the secrets of Asklepios, learn from the shamans, adopt the wisdom of traditional Chinese doctors, study spiritual healing, and discover the secrets of the soul and its relation to the body? Medicine would become much bigger, and grand egos would appear as nothing in comparison. What if we fought to keep the knowledge of the Amazon River people, their use of plants and their rituals? What if we studied Paracelsus, the extraordinary physician of 16th-century Europe who used alchemy and said confidently that there is no disease that doesn't have a cure? He also said that every illness has a wife, its remedy.

Traditional societies recognize a medicine man or woman as a spiritual leader. Lacking that expansive vision of human life, we allow doctors a generally well-paying and prestigious job. We fall short. Money doesn't adequately substitute for spiritual standing. But how do we change? Is it possible to once again become a spiritual culture?

Lacking pervasive spirituality, we reduce it to competing belief systems, a serious reduction of religion to opinion rather than spiritual wisdom and openness, and top-heavy, authoritarian religious institutions. Ask a person about his religion and he will most likely tell you what organization he belongs to, what he believes, or what church he goes to. He won't talk about his methods of contemplation or his service to humanity. He won't mention his calling in life or the things he does to be ethical and visionary. Today people think of religion as a thing, an institution. Many therefore drop the word *religion* and use *spirituality* instead.

The typical Western well-educated man or woman— say, a doctor or nurse—may not have much room for religion in his or her life. Science explains nature and human behavior. Ethics is a simple notion of right and wrong. Life is busy and full on a purely secular level. For that person, religion probably means a naïve belief system coupled to a church, and church-going is fairly dull, repetitious, and irrelevant. Of course, there are many exceptions, but the churches are not full these days. A recent report indicated a 10 percent drop in church attendance over ten years in the United States.

My field is religion, and I am biased. But at the very least, religion to me means rich traditions containing powerful stories, teachings, thinkers, and rituals that keep life tethered to the deepest sensitivities and values. You don't have to join a church or temple or religious institution of any kind to benefit seriously from a study of religious traditions. My life wouldn't be the same without Zen Buddhism, but I am not a Buddhist. All my actions find their guidance from the Tao Te Ching, the central text of Chinese Taoism. But I'm not a Taoist. In many ways I am deeply Catholic, but my connection to the Catholic Church is tenuous at this point in my life. In all this, I consider myself a strong religious person.

If doctors and nurses are going to become more spiritual in their work, they will have to discover a deeper meaning to religion and spirituality. They will have to go beyond passive participation in rote church services and shallow requirements of ethics. Medicine challenges us all with questions not only about what we should not do, but positively what we should contribute to the world community. The woman I mentioned who was celibate for two years before beginning her medical practice was doing so on her own. She was borrowing a traditional practice, but no one told her to do it. You can imagine that her life in medicine will not be troubled by arrogance.

One day I visited a hospital where I had heard they had a program in spirituality and medicine. I inquired about it and was told, "Oh, yes, we have an acupuncturist coming once a week." I happen to appreciate acupuncture very much, but acupuncture doesn't define a program in spirituality and medicine.

I don't know how to reach the level of spiritual and religious sophistication we need in order to bring medicine up out of its limiting secularism. It's difficult to teach these subjects in school because people are so sensitive about their beliefs. They don't understand that a teacher can present the basics of a religion without trying to convert a student. Unfortunately, some teachers don't understand that distinction either. Popular books and workshop leaders usually offer a sentimental view of spirituality, and so they don't help either. Still, culture can go through major changes when the spirit of the times makes a slight shift. We have made progress with sexism, racism, and environmental awareness; maybe we can also deepen our general sense of religion and spirituality.

I define religion at its core as standing on the edge of your existence, open to the future, open to what life has to offer, open to need in your community, and open as you live from your heart. You can do this as a liberal Catholic, an evangelical Christian, a Buddhist, a Muslim, or an atheist. If you are focused on yourself and living in a world encased in complete control and explanation, bereft of mystery, then no matter how often you go to church, you have no religion in the sense I am defining it.

It takes a big vision to live with such a vast spiritual sensibility, but the average person today doesn't get an education, either in school or in church, that prepares him for it. Religion is reduced to belief, and spirituality to personal achievement in meditation, psychology, and yoga. Yet a rich spiritual education would be more compatible with the highly sophisticated technical education that doctors and nurses get in their training.

When I was a young man, I studied the theology of Thomas Aquinas in Latin for almost six years. In his day, the 13th century, theology was the most sophisticated subject you could study, and theologians enjoyed the reputation of being brilliant thinkers. Today, just about the reverse is true. Theology seems naïve and is allied to simplistic belief. Even in Aquinas's time and later, a physician might study theology as the crowning course of his education. The famous physician Paracelsus writes as a theologian about concrete medical matters. Whatever it would take to return theological thinking to medicine—not sectarian or defensive thinking—would increase a doctor's vision and help him or her be a person of great vision in the practice of medicine. That development could be a solution to the problem of sadomasochism and arrogance in the profession.

The Divine Marquis

How does this excursion into spirituality apply to the problem of arrogance and the Sadean side of medicine? Recall the image of the Lapis Lazuli Radiant Healing Buddha and the Native American medicine man adorned in a halo of bright feathers. These are figures of spiritual power. I believe that Sade was trying to reveal the spiritual power needed to survive as a human being in a challenging world and unmasking all the abuse and symptomatic forms of power that we would now call sadomasochistic.

If doctors or nurses were to embrace the full spiritual dimension of their calling, they might not have such a need to exercise power over other people. Domination is a symptomatic form of spiritual power. A dominating, arrogant person exploits his position to control others for his own neurotic need. He lacks the spiritual vision and maturity to measure up to his calling and therefore can't summon up the deep authority of his life work.

Some professions appeal to people with power complexes—teaching, police work, politics, and medicine, for example. Some people readily play the victim to these professionals. They suffer through a long and arduous education. They get in trouble with the law. They go too far in submitting to government demands. They tremble in the presence of a surgeon. Patients and professionals may both find themselves at one end or the other of a power complex.

One way out of, or better, through the power complex is to allow spiritual power to move through you, not stay glued to your ego, where your own needs get in the way. A modern-day doctor has the gift of centuries of medical research and discovery in him. He did not make all those discoveries. He could use them humbly and not pump his ego with his knowledge. He could go out of the way to honor those who came before him.

The modern doctor could also understand the limits of knowledge and allow for the mysterious even in the most technical forms of treatment. I once assisted Dr. Michael Kearney, author of the insightful book *Mortally Wounded,* in a medical class at McGill University in Montreal. We were in the center of the lecture hall, surrounded by a semicircle of medical faculty. I remember one doctor, upon hearing us talk about mystery, saying that she often feels that a patient is healed when she turns her back. That image struck me. It was her way of saying that amid all our high-tech know-how and methods, a mysterious element still plays a role in healing. This doctor said that she appreciated discussing the issue and finding intelligent language for it.

A modern doctor could also develop a practice of meditation, suited to his temperament, in which he could reflect regularly on matters of illness, health, recovery, and death. He could develop a life of prayer, again suited to his personal style and intellectual life. Many highly trained people know prayer and other spiritual practices only in naïve forms and therefore dismiss them. An alternative is to become more sophisticated about these practices, weaving them seamlessly into a life of highly skilled medical work.

In this way the professional develops confidence and power, free of ego limitations, rooted instead in a large vision and in a practice of considering the ultimate issues that face every human being. This kind of practice offers both deep personal power and a religious way of acknowledging power beyond one's own capacities. This is a good method for resolving the sadomasochistic issues that weaken the practice of medicine.

CHAPTER 11

THE SOUL
OF FOOD

Whenever I have visited friends and family members in a hospital, I've noticed that often the first thing other visitors say is, "How's the food?"

Food has many layers of meaning and significance. It is a basic human need and most everyone is interested in it from some point of view. It's our common denominator; it establishes our connection to each other and offers a safe and engaging subject to talk about. We all know something about food, and many of us know how to obtain it, cook it, present it, and enjoy it.

You can consider food's role in health as nourishment. You can think of it as representing cultures and ethnic groups. It can be the focus of intimate conversation, big parties, and many other kinds of human interaction. It can be used as medicine. Avoiding it, you can think about it in terms of a diet, or an anorexic fantasy of not being solidly on the earth, or fasting from it as a way to be spiritually virtuous. Fantasies about food are florid and far-ranging.

As a child I grew up with simple food. Today, I think of that fare as being Midwestern and 1950-ish. I had cereal for breakfast, lunch-meat sandwiches at noon, and meat and potatoes at night. I never thought much about food as related to my health, and I never heard of health food.

In my 40s, with hypertension and a hypothyroid-inspired tendency to gain weight, I began to watch my food more carefully. Generally I avoided a fatty diet and ate a small lunch and an ordinary supper. As a child I had always drunk fruit juice and eaten every kind of fruit I could find. I remember that my mother liked to cook salmon patties— the fish always coming from a can—calf's liver, brussels sprouts, roast beef and potatoes, and a very plain spaghetti with meat sauce. She liked to have several vegetables, more than fully cooked, and cottage cheese and coleslaw on the table. There was also a drawer in the kitchen that was always full of cookies that I would sample throughout the day. Some would say that it's no surprise that I have heart disease today.

In my late 40s, when I met my wife, Joan Hanley, who is an artist and trainer of Kundalini yoga teachers, I discovered a completely foreign approach to food. For a while I wondered if food might be an obstacle to us getting married. She introduced me to vegetarianism, tofu, and a few ugly meat substitutes. She drinks gallons of water each day, eats fruit and nuts for breakfast, has her big meal at noon, and likes sourdough breads full of seeds and smelling like the farm where I spent summers as a child. I still love white bread, although I have progressed beyond the pale soft loaves I enjoyed when I was young.

We raised our children in a big house that we built on a hill in New Hampshire. A quarter of a mile down the road was a biodynamic farm (organic plus) where we were members and for many years had fresh vegetables and dairy products any time we wanted them. I've grown to love vegetarian meals and fresh wholesome food, and I enjoy cooking food that is healthy and delicious.

I am also a confirmed Epicurean. That means that I believe in a life of simple pleasures, like friends and food. Epicurus was an early Greek philosopher who advocated pleasure in moderation. He was a vegetarian who loved to gather friends and eat well. My mentors, writers about soul over the centuries, tend to be Epicureans as well: Marsilio Ficino, Oscar Wilde, C. G. Jung, and James Hillman, to name a few. In my books I sometimes make the case that Jesus, too, was an Epicurean. One of the reasons I like to be in Ireland so much is because of the high degree of Epicurean sophistication I see cultivated there.

While the spirit often finds joy in limiting food and giving it a sparse quality, the soul enjoys indulging in food and drink. In relation to health, medicine, and hospital life, I try to keep these two inclinations in mind, like yin and yang, one influencing and qualifying the other.

Preparing for this book, I spoke with dieticians and food-service managers in hospitals. In the privacy of my thoughts I was looking for evidence of soul in this area, although no one I spoke to had a similar bias. Most were interested in food as medicine. They counted calories closely, watched for fat in the diets of certain patients, and squirted nutritional chemicals into food that would otherwise be bland and useless.

When my mother was in her last months in a convalescent home, one day they put a feeding tube into her. They told us she would die very soon if we didn't allow it. Now my father and I wish we had not supported this procedure that caused my mother considerable discomfort. I spoke with the dietician treating her, and he was interested only in the chemical components of the food my mother was eating. While she was in the home, this important human activity that had been so much a part of her life disappeared in the name of health.

I've always had mixed feelings about so-called health food. When the fantasy behind it is either chemical or depriving, I avoid it as much as I can. A palpable moralism easily creeps into our feelings about food, and we may feel virtuous for depriving ourselves of the pleasures food offers. I am for careful eating without moralism. Healthy food is no doubt good for your body, but moralism is bad for your soul. Many times I have stood at a table laid out with a variety of foods and heard people use moral words like "sinful" and "tempting" for foods they would like to eat but avoid because of their ideas of health. You may feel sinful if you eat sweets and chocolate or meat or fried foods.

I find special pleasure in eating food that is good for me and at the same time tastes good and is beautifully presented. A highly spiritual person might appreciate a Spartan approach to dinner, but a person with soul will want a beautiful experience of food that offers pleasure at many levels—looks, presentation, taste, camaraderie, stories, good lighting, and a beautiful table and dinnerware.

While in the hospital for a heart procedure, I was in a desperately sparse and unattractive room, but I did have a room-service style of dining. I was given a menu early in the day and I could call for my food whenever I wanted it. One hospital food manager with whom I spoke said that this is an ideal for many hospitals, but it is generally too expensive, requiring a complicated plan of service and a way to deal with food waste. Still, I might choose a hospital that gave its food service some grace, interest, beauty, and human satisfaction rather than mere health benefit. If a hospital is going to heal the soul as well as the body, the way it deals with food is crucial, because food lies at the center of soul life.

I discovered this truth when I first published *Care of the Soul*. I went out on long tours for this book, expecting to talk theology and philosophy. Instead, everywhere I went the issue of food kept coming up, either in my own thoughts or from audiences. Back then I was advocating "slow food" and Epicureanism. I often asked an audience: If you're having trouble with your marriage or a romantic relationship, do you call a friend and say, "I know an empty space where we can discuss this," or do you say, "Let's have lunch"?

Food nurtures not only the body but the soul and spirit as well. Thinking of the years of raising my children on fresh organic-farm food, I asked an inner-city hospital food manager why her hospital still offers so many bland puddings on its menu. "We can put nutrients in those puddings," she said.

"I'd rather have a banana," I responded.

"You can have a banana for breakfast. We can give you that."

"I'd like some organic food. Doesn't it make sense that in a hospital, of all places, pure foods rich in nutrients would be the basis of a menu?"

"Too expensive. We couldn't consider it," she said.

"What about a restaurant-style menu and room service?"

"We'd love to do that, but we can't afford it."

The impression I took away from my meeting with the hospital food manager was that food must be low on the list of priorities among the hospital leaders. I attended a luncheon at the hospital where very expensive food was served to patrons being asked to help purchase a new machine. Money seems to go for machines but not for food. For the modernist/materialist/mechanical notion of treatment, but not for the soul.

Dining Versus Feeding Time

A few years ago I participated in a program sponsored by the Irish Hospice Foundation. Our meeting took place in a hotel at the Dublin Airport and included some excellent talks. One theme that inspired the meeting was a problem among elderly men and women living in the country-side. They typically refused to leave home for the hospital because of their attachment to home and their fear or dis-taste for life away from it.

We are dealing here with a deep feeling of security and comfort and connectedness to home—not necessarily the literal house, but a sense of being at home. You can never completely overcome the loss of home when a patient stays at a hospital, but you could bridge it. One way is to take care and use a sensitive imagination in preparing and serv-ing food. It was a small thing, that day in the hospital when I was handed a menu, but it meant a great deal. Then I could associate being in a hospital with being in a hotel. Because of my work of lecturing and book touring, I spend a lot of my life in hotels, and generally I enjoy it. I'd much rather see a hospital as a hotel than as an institution for treating my body with chemicals and machines.

Hotel and *hospital* come from the same root word, which means "guest." *Hospitality* and *hospital* are almost the same word, and rightly so. Maybe it would be better to speak of patients in a hospital as "guests." The first job of a hospital would be to offer hospitality rather than to give the impression that every kind of smelly chemical and gro-tesque machine is going to be used on your body, whether you like it or not, because the prime directive of doctors and nurses is to keep you alive and certainly not to make you comfortable.

A hotel is a home away from home; maybe a hospi-tal should also try to offer a sense of home, even though it will never be a literal home. "Home" is an archetypal experience, meaning a deep sensation that may or may not arise from an actual house. You may feel more at home in a friend's house than the house of your parents or the one in which you grew up.

Since home is archetypal, it can be evoked in various places, including a hospital, and food is a significant aspect of the experience of home.

Another story I often tell concerns a man who once called in on a talk-radio show I was doing with my friend Jean Feraca from Madison, Wisconsin. Our topic was food, and this man called to say that he had moved to Wisconsin from the South and was having trouble adjusting. He had been depressed. One day he said to a friend back home he was phoning, "All they eat here is cheese." The friend sent him some normal food from home, including grits, and immediately the depression lifted. Home and food go together.

Other soul ingredients go into food, such as memory. Nothing is more satisfying than to have some food cooked exactly the way you remember it from your childhood or from a pleasurable trip. When you are in the hospital, you live on your memories. Home and your normal life are at a distance and temporarily inaccessible. It would help to have some food that you know well and that conjures up your everyday life.

Some hospitals provide kitchens where you can cook food that you know in ways that are familiar to you. Cooking itself can restore your life to you and make you feel like a human being once more.

Beyond home and memory, food well cooked and presented can give you the feeling of living a cultured life. Too many things in a hospital make you think about survival rather than beautiful and graceful living. The survival mentality goes along with the idea that you are a collection of body parts in need of repair, rather than a human being. Just a little grace and beauty raises the level of life several notches.

Attention to food is often the spur to graciousness in other areas. Doctors, nurses, and various attendants might be inspired to speak more graciously and conduct themselves with style if they had a gracious place in which to have lunch. The factory mentality comes not only from architecture and décor that is excessively pragmatic and lacking in beauty, but also from the manner in which people behave. If you conceive of illness as a malfunctioning set of organs, you will create an atmosphere that is equally primitive.

When I was in my 20s, my doctor put me in the hospital for two weeks for mononucleosis. It was a charming hospital in an affluent suburb of Chicago. I still remember the cloth napkins, the glass of red wine, and the superb menu. I know that most hospitals can't afford such luxury, but any effort toward civilized dining would help the atmosphere.

Food and Personality

Food is at least as important for the personality as it is for the body. By "personality" I mean everything that goes into being a person. There is the old saying that "you are what you eat." I prefer to say, "You are the way you eat." If you really dine, taking care with the preparation of your food, the choice of what you eat, the environment, the presentation, the accoutrements—plates, décor, chairs, table, glasses, cutlery—your experience could be a genuinely soulful one.

This is true wherever and whenever you eat. Care creates the conditions in which soul can appear. It is especially important in a hospital, when life has been stripped to its essentials. Eating is a focal point of the day. How you eat, what you eat, the situation in which you eat make all the difference.

In hospitals, a patient tends to eat alone, and that is fine much of the time. When you're sick, you may not feel very sociable. But once in a while it might be good to have the opportunity to eat with others, including the staff. I'm reminded of my experience of teaching at Schumacher College in Devon, England. Founded by Satish Kumar, this is a humane kind of educational setting, where students and faculty and staff all prepare the food and eat together. It's what an anthropologist might call commensality—people of different backgrounds sitting at the same table (*mensa*).

At Schumacher College commensality helps create community. It breaks down some of the barriers between classes of workers, students, and teachers. This could be useful in a hospital, where boundaries do become barriers and a class system rules. Patients are part of this social arrangement and could benefit from eating together with other patients and staff. On the other hand, doctors may also benefit from eating with doctors and nurses with nurses. What I have seen in hospitals is a form of multitasking—nurses eat on the fly in small, cluttered rooms used for meetings, phone calls, arguments, and lunch.

Satish Kumar always says that he built his schools around lunch. His schools are not only successful; they are full of warmth, community, and engagement. A hospital could also take its food and dining seriously—not only patients' food but food for the staff as well.

Food and Self-Care

When you're sick at home, you might also take note of the power of food to heal and sustain the soul. Food is an important step toward healing, not only at the physical level, but for the soul and spirit, too. Even if you don't feel like eating or if you're on a restricted diet, you can still dine. You can sit at the table with friends and loved ones. The soul will benefit.

Understanding the importance to health of food and dining, when you get sick you might make an effort to eat with some style. Sometimes illness brings out an attitude of

Spartan self-denial. Maybe there is a fantasy of punishment in the background, or an attempt to give up pleasure in a deal with fate or God to get better. You may have to counter that unconscious wish and bring more style (Aphrodite) into life.

Remember Epicurus, an admirable philosopher. He recommended simple pleasures especially during an illness. You might find some favorite foods and keep them handy as you recover. You might even cheat on your diet once in a while, just to keep any floating moralism at bay.

Good food is the gift of Demeter, the mother of life, who wants us to thrive, even though in the end we all return to her. There is no option but to honor Mother Earth when we are sick, and one way to do that is to eat her simple, natural foods, prepared with care and style. Good food is her gift to humanity, and we are asked to receive it with a pure and open heart.

CHAPTER 12

RESPECT
FOR THE BODY

As Western culture began to shift from religion and magic to science in the 17th century, the soul began to leave the Western body, and with its loss the body became an object rather than a presence. Gradually we lost respect for the body because it no longer offered contact with the soul. It became lifeless and therefore shrunk in value.

The disrespect we're talking about has roots in the history of medicine, when the focus on anatomy, the body as corpse, and its breakup into systems and parts weakened the feeling for the body as part of the personality. From the point of view of medical history, it may seem like an advance to look at the body and see anatomy, but from the perspective of the soul something essential was lost.

If you regard the body as a thing, you will have less respect for it than if you see it as the presentation of a person in context and in relationship. Bernd Jager, a professor of depth psychology I knew many years ago, has studied this development and talks about a "situated body." You place a body on a chart or translate it into a collection of plastic parts, and you have taken away the situation every human body is in. We don't live in abstract space. We're not people on a page. We live in a certain place and work in a particular building or town and with certain people. But medicine pictures its body unsituated, outside of any context, amenable to charts and models having removable parts.

It's difficult for modern medicine to see a connection between the heart that pumps blood and the one we put on a valentine card. Yet our language about being heartfelt, having a broken heart, speaking from the heart, and having a heart-to-heart conversation makes it clear beyond any doubt that the heart is, in some real sense, the seat of deep emotion. If you think this is only a matter of metaphor, then you don't appreciate the depth and power of images.

Professor Jager also points to the difference between the medical body and the psychoanalytic body. Freud's body was a body of desire, focused particularly on the mouth, the sexual organs, and the anus, each representing a certain longing and pleasure. The mouth has memories of sucking the mother's breast, with feelings of comfort and eventually withdrawal.[27] Imagine treating sores on the mouth with an awareness of its important role in the psychological life of the patient.

Some get annoyed with the extreme detail of psychoanalytic readings of the body, but we can take the general point easily: the body is a symbolic body. The body as a whole and in each part reveals the soul and says something meaningful about the person. These meanings have impact and effect beneath the level of consciousness. They are buried in our language, our thoughts, and our behavior.

Isn't it remarkable that Freud pored over the symbolism of the mouth and especially its role in infancy, and then late in life contracted cancer of the mouth? I have not been able to find studies on this matter, although a few analysts have noted a connection between a major dream of Freud's, presented in detail in his pioneering work *The Interpretation of Dreams,* and his cancer. "Irma's dream" was about doctors treating a woman who had white scabs on her mouth. Freud's report of his dream sounds almost exactly like reports of his cancer symptoms. Dream specialist Robert Moss wonders if Freud should have seen his dream in less dogmatic terms and taken a warning about his health.[28]

I already mentioned a student of mine who had a chronic sore throat and imagined broken glass in that part of her body. The human body is full of memories and images that have an impact on the emotions and are implicated somehow in our illnesses. Seeing the body this way, as profoundly expressive of a patient's personal past and deep emotions, might help a health-care worker give the person more respect.

A nurse doing an intake assessment for me at a medical clinic once measured me in my bare feet and, looking at a record of my medical history, pronounced that I had shrunk. She laughed at me saying that I probably didn't know I was getting shorter. Now, most people like to stand tall. We don't like being told that we're shrinking, and we especially don't like being laughed at for our human frailty. I think that this nurse was just trying to be friendly, but the way she laughed made me feel humiliated. I never went back to that place.

This sounds like pride, and it is. Patients have an inborn, essential pride. They don't need or want to be humiliated, and there is every opportunity in medicine to humiliate. Professionals could be more sensitive to these issues and go beyond what is necessary to assure a person's pride and dignity. Since illness and the medical culture already put people in a humble place of suffering and passivity, they need an added measure of assurance and positive recognition.

Disrespect is often due simply to unconsciousness. Health-care workers go about their duties focused on the well-being of their patients and never think about such things as pride, dignity, and self-worth. Unconsciously they may offend and hurt patients, making the overall experience of medicine a humiliating one.

I Am a Person

These days, when you enter a hospital for treatment, the person doing the intake places a band around your wrist with your name and some number for identification. It is useful to the hospital and its staff for keeping patients straight. You don't want to treat one person for another person's complaint. Still, there is something impersonal about these ID tags. For all the useful information it contains, and in spite of the safety it offers, the wristband is like a band on a steer's ear, turning him into a useful item on the assembly line.

These days it is tempting to study the body's quantitative readouts rather than look at the body itself. I go to my doctor and we sit in front of his computer, checking levels of various chemicals in the blood. These are more than useful and certainly have a place. Fortunately my doctor can do both, look at my body and check the numbers. But I've known other doctors who don't bother with an examination once they have their numbers.

I remember the night my daughter was born. It was Thanksgiving and the staff at the hospital was minimal. My wife and I were on our own, for the most part. A nurse set us up in a birthing room and showed us how to read the data that machines were giving out in a continuous read of glowing numbers. I kept trying to watch the signs on my wife's body, but I had to work at withdrawing my attention from the machines and their readouts. I wanted to be with my wife, not with data issuing from her body.

We have to make some fairly easy judgments in dealing with persons. Of course, it's useful to have data about a patient, and radio-equipped or bar-coded wristbands make a lot of sense. In one hospital I visited, wristbands allowed a patient to get an X-ray with no waiting at all. That would seem to be progress. But everything, including our wisest inventions and protocols, has a shadow side, and we could address that as well. If a wristband makes a person feel like a collection of numbers, then why not give the band some individuality, personality, and soul—a drawing, photo, philosophy, quotation, song, animal, tree, or food type?

The problem occurs in other areas of life. As an altar boy, I always found it odd when a priest would say a funeral Mass and get the name of the dead person wrong, as one did with an uncle of mine. Or at a wedding, the priest would sometimes hesitate when it came to the names of the people getting married, or he'd have to take out a sheet of paper from his vest pocket before continuing. Would it be that difficult to get to know the people on whose lives you are about to have a critical impact?

Technical advances have a way of putting the human and the personal further back into the shadows. A surgeon enters a hospital room and beholds a jungle of wires and tubes and reads a chart and notes the wristband. Where is the person in all of this? Hiding behind the technology. As a patient, you want to say: "Hey, I'm here. I'm not the sum total of my data and numbers and printouts. I have a life and a personality. I'm a person."

I have a friend, Brother Henry, a member of a Catholic religious order, who has a heart as wide as a continent. Once, he had to spend extended time in a hospital after knee surgery. At the time, I was well into the writing of this book, and I asked him to relate his observations to me.

He said that one of his frustrations was having nurses and doctors and technicians coming to his room one after the other. None of them gave the others information about the patient. So Brother Henry had to keep repeating all the data. Finally, feeling like a battered object rather than a human being, in his own fashion he called a meeting of his caretakers. He didn't berate them but charmed them. He got them interested in him as a person. He showed them who he was. He was funny with them and warm. After that, he said, he was treated like a special person.

Not only patients, but certain staff members, like nurses, become objects, if they enjoy any visibility at all. In one emergency room at a large hospital, the director told me that under the previous regime nurses were so invisible, so ignored, and so slighted that the turnover rate was unacceptable. It took just a few thoughtful changes in protocol to reverse the situation in a matter of months. Introducing soul to a hospital is quick, simple, and inexpensive. It's worth trying.

The director told me that he set up a simple rule: no second-guessing. If a nurse or technician made a decision and offered a certain treatment according to protocols, the doctors should not question or challenge the decision but rather investigate the protocols with the director. He was trying to save underlings the embarrassment of having their judgment questioned in front of other staff and patients. One would think that could be a no-brainer.

Here, too, is another obvious point that I heard discussed in every hospital I visited: a nurse is a person deserving of respect. People tend to think of nurses as extensions of the doctors and not having a position and role of their own. Part of the problem is no doubt a subtle and long-standing sexism, since most nurses are women. People look at a hospital staff and see women doing the kind of chores a mother might do in a family and the doctor being the father. Thus, there are two problems in one: the failure to understand the professional education and abilities of a nurse, and a tendency to denigrate the role of feminine care of patients. Nurses are *only* doing the ongoing care of the patient, while the doctors are offering highly technical treatments.

Bernd Jager used the term "theatricality" to describe the dress and manner that doctors sometimes take on. There is also theater in the way nurses take care of patients hour by hour and in constant proximity, while the doctor appears as the expert from outside. Nurses' theater is more homely and intimate and therefore may be taken for granted. This theater may have to change somewhat before nurses will get the respect due to them.

One of the most remarkable interviews I did, accompanied by Mark McKinney and Sharon O'Brien, at a large city hospital was with a nurse manager who had sorted out her calling, her values, her career, and her profession more than anyone else I encountered. She worked on a cardiology floor and spoke of the challenge of inspiring and leading nurses doing demanding and highly specialized work.

Without thinking, I "led the witness" by saying that she must find this hospital a special place and particularly good for her career. "Not really," she said. "I've been in other places where nurses have more respect and where they can do their professional work without constant interference and oversight. This hospital doesn't trust its nurses," she said, "and so I try extra hard in my role as nurse manager to inspire and respect my nurses."

This woman was confident, very bright, and apparently fearless. She told how she had gone to considerable trouble to get this job in order to work with a doctor whose brilliance she admired. I left the interview thinking that if only every department of every hospital had a clone of this nurse, many problems would be solved.

Many nurses told us that doctors and patients often don't realize how important *care,* in addition to treatment, is in the healing of a patient. Most of the material in medical journals and hospital publications is about technical treatments instead. We don't seem to understand either the importance or the potential sophistication of care. The emotional life requires its own kind of intelligence and expertise, and I don't mean to say that it should be reduced to research methods and quantitative formulations. It can be done through intelligence about how to be human, not mechanical.

The Doctor as Medicine Man

Let's return briefly to the image of the stethoscope hooked around a doctor's neck and shoulders. This is part of the theater of doctoring today. A shaman medicine man may have a necklace of beads or shells around his neck, partly for the sound it makes as he walks and moves. A shaman gains access to the Otherworld, where the roots of healing are to be found, by shaking a rattle, making a strong and piercing sound. The modern doctor also has a sound device around his neck, but his is quiet. Instead of making noise, the stethoscope amplifies the heartbeat and other internal bodily noises.

As is often the case in modern culture, the quest for the Otherworld turns into a search in the literal, physical, internal realm of the body. The stethoscope replaces the rattle, and its symbolic importance in recognizing the office of doctor remains as a vestige and is used unconsciously. It's interesting and relevant that when relatives are looking for a gift to give a graduating medical student, they often choose a stethoscope.

The shift from bones and beads to the stethoscope around the neck represents a profound difference in worldview and culture. The modern doctor has become a technician and bases his or her practice on a long and demanding education in science. The theatrical use of the stethoscope hints at an earlier sensibility but, being but a vestige, it doesn't offer much to the doctor beyond pride and a little power among persons.

This may all sound like anthropological lore of no practical value. My point is that today a doctor yearns for the soul gift of respect because he himself has lost sight of the spiritual aspect of his calling and work. It is ultimately self-defeating to be in a sacred profession while cultivating a persona that is completely secular. Secularism is a form of soul loss.

The medicine man of primal societies always has with him (or her) many signs of the spiritual nature of his work. The neckwear allows him to summon the Otherworld or protect himself from it. He may carry a drum on which is painted the multilayered universe in which he works and lives. These drums often have lines drawn across them, distinguishing an upper world from an underworld and then from the ordinary plane of our daily existence.

He may wear feathers, signs of his ability to fly between these different worlds, or the image of a ladder to indicate his ability to move among them. He is aware of the symbolic meaning and importance of these images, and they in turn help sustain his awareness. The modern doctor, in contrast, wears his stethoscope theatrically but has no serious intention with regard to its symbolism.

The doctor's situation is similar to that of the artist in our secular society. Generally we have lost our appreciation for the role of the arts in the life of the soul. We've lost sight of the soul altogether, for that matter. So instead of understanding how important art objects are for the sustenance of our souls, we now value art primarily for its monetary worth. Today people look at a painting and say, "I wonder how much that's worth."

A doctor, who by vocation is dealing with life and death and the sacred human body, deserves vast respect for his role in the community. But if he sees himself only as a technician, as applying science to people, he will have little grounds for respect. He will be treated as a technician, which is far from his spiritual calling.

Here is the root of the doctor's depression, dissatisfaction, and burnout: the gulf between the inherent spiritual value of his calling and the secular way he is educated and carries on his work.

There is no escaping the sacredness of the body and the mysteriousness of illness. The doctor, try as he might, can't avoid the profundity of birth, illness, and death—all directly within the purview of his work. The secularism of modern medicine may distract from these sacred values, but it can't entirely cover them up. So the doctor suffers the enormous gap between his exalted calling and the secular trappings of the modern profession.

Of all the doctors with whom I spoke, two kinds stood out as especially happy and fulfilled in their work—family physicians and pediatric oncologists. This discovery was a surprise to me. I thought that family medicine would be too ordinary to be interesting, but it seems that the medical involvement with people over the span of their lives, dealing with marriages and children and the elderly, offers special satisfactions. I also expected working with children's cancer to be emotionally exhausting. But I found doctors and nurses in this area deeply satisfied and fulfilled. Most said that they were inspired by the positive and mature attitudes of the children they served.

In both of these areas in medicine the soul issues come out strong. To work with families and deal with children in the face of death asks something personal and deep from the health-care worker. In return, the worker sees far past his job and understands a deeper role he plays in the lives of others.

I don't expect us to go back to primal ways and see doctors wearing feathers and beads. It is not a bad idea, but it isn't going to happen. Still, a doctor could cultivate his own spiritual life in ways that would give his work its needed verticality—its depth and transcendence. We have already seen some ways that the professional can become more spiritually sophisticated. Here's another list: The doctor could meditate regularly, pray, do special work for the community, treat his profession as a spiritual calling, go on regular retreats, keep track of his dreams, study the world's spiritual traditions, read sacred texts, learn alternative methods of treatment and systems of healing, paint or play music, do sculpture or dance or photography, cook, travel, hike, or write poetry. A doctor could cultivate a spiritual life for himself and then let that spiritual sensibility color his work in medicine.

Small things also help keep the spiritual in mind: displaying a statue of a healing figure like Quan Yin, the Buddha, or a saint; posting a quote that captures the idea briefly and powerfully; or wearing a certain color or keeping an object nearby that reminds the doctor of his spiritual calling. Rings, pendants, shawls, pins, head coverings— these simple objects have extraordinary potency and can help sustain a spiritual outlook.

Early in my career I made a close study of European Renaissance books on healing and good living. I was especially drawn to Marsilio Ficino, a magus, astrologer, physician, musician, and theologian of the 1400s. He wrote books about using objects to create a powerful life and environment and specifically recommended taking care with colors and jewelry and objects in your home or work setting. Ficino stands out in Western history as a master of soul-making, and he has much to teach about being a soul-centered and spiritual healer. He would have been fascinated with the current symbolic use of the stethoscope and other similar symbols of the medical professional.

He said that images should be striking and have an impact on anyone who sees them. I once visited the building in the Florence suburbs where Ficino taught. Today there are still fascinating statues in the garden, much in the spirit of Ficino. One in particular I remember of an old man with a baby's body and claw feet riding a turtle. This is an old symbol of reconciling youth and old age, speed and slowness.

In the room where I do therapy, my place of healing, I have a healing figure in black stone from the Northwest native people, a statue of Asklepios, one of Saint Thomas More, and several paintings by my wife, one in particular on the theme of Daphne and Apollo and another of the Buddha entering Nirvana. I also have a soapstone statue of the laughing Buddha. He reminds me always to bring a light spirit as well as profound thoughts to my spirituality and my work. This, too, is a form of respect for the body. People often complain that Western societies are materialistic, and that is true to a point. But it would help to understand that materialism is a complex, a neurosis. That is what "ism" on a word usually means. In this case, it means that we have a bad relationship to the material world, including physical things and the human body. We are neurotic about the world's body as well as the human body.

The tendency I already mentioned of looking at quantified printouts instead of the actual body is one way we go for the abstraction rather than the physical thing. Medicine might improve if it could develop a deeper appreciation for the physical body and things in general. It isn't enough to have a hospital that functions well. It also has to be beautiful and comforting. It isn't enough to have a hospital room with all the latest technology; it also has to be homelike and cozy.

Respect for the body doesn't mean, then, just an honoring of a patient's body, but a deep appreciation for the physical life—the symbolic richness of certain objects; the value of old objects, such as antiques, to keep memory alive; the beauty of an orchid placed on a simple but elegant table in an otherwise barren corner.

Daphne Resisting

I mentioned that among the valued objects in the room where I write is a painting by my wife of Daphne. Let's digress for a moment on this myth because it has relevance to our theme of the abstract versus the physical.

Daphne is a young virgin spirit, a minor version of the great goddess of the pristine forest, Artemis, known to the ancient Romans as Diana. One day the god Apollo spots her, and Eros shoots a flaming arrow of passion into his heart. He goes after her, literally chases her. She runs away. As they are running, Apollo shouts: "I am the Lord of Delphi. I make music wherever it happens. I invented medicine." But Daphne is not impressed. It is not in her nature to be linked to a man. She runs faster and calls out for help from her father, a river spirit. Immediately she begins to change into a tree, as leaves sprout from the branches of her arms and her legs root into the earth.

Women often hear this story as a plain tale about men chasing them and trying to dominate them. That is certainly one level at which this story has meaning for us. But literary tradition takes the story deeper. I used to tell it to university students, who, much like Diana in their innocence, didn't want to be taught or enculturated. Something in them, a Daphne spirit, resisted the loss of their natural innocence.

The same may be true of patients under the care of doctors. It was Apollo, after all, who fathered Asklepios, the god of medicine. Maybe there is something in patients that doesn't want to be treated, that backs away from the urgent need of medicine to heal at all costs. Maybe there is a precious natural soul that doesn't want to subject itself to healing practices. Doctors and nurses can sometimes be frustrated by what they sense as *resistance* in their patients. I might call that resistance Daphne.

A patient won't take his medicine or otherwise comply with instructions. The doctor or nurse may be evoking Apollo by insisting, humanely of course, that the patient follow directions. Doctors notoriously use language for patient noncompliance that suggests the Daphne effect.

"The patient *denies* fatigue," a report will say. Denies? That's a strong word for natural resistance to treatment.

A doctor's need to help and to heal sometimes goes beyond what is reasonable. Sometimes the doctor's need to heal is stronger than the patient's need to be healed. A patient may sense the doctor's need and, perhaps unconsciously, resists it. I sometimes feel like Daphne when people have a need to help me even when I don't want their help. It's a similar pattern in medicine: the doctor's vocation is to help a person get better, and so he sometimes gets carried away.

The patient's impulse to resist is not always the doctor's doing. For many reasons, a patient may not be amenable to medical help. He doesn't want a doctor messing with him, even with the high motive of healing.

It's common for people to become aware of symptoms but put off going to the doctor because they don't want the doctor's expert diagnosis. They don't want to subject themselves to the system. They know that once they enter the doctor's office, they are setting themselves up for tests, treatments, consultations, and bad news. They'd rather remain in the limbo of uncertainty. I felt this way when I first noticed pains in my back that turned out to be angina. Daphne goes natural and runs away. At first, I waited to see if the symptoms would just go away. I turned into a tree.

Health-care workers know that patients are often reluctant to face their illnesses and tell a doctor everything he wants to know. The professionals judge it as a weakness of character or mere ignorance. But the pattern may be archetypal, simply something that human beings do, often without much consciousness.

Doctors and nurses may have to learn to respect the body's reluctance to be probed, tested, and treated. This attitude on the part of a patient may not come from ignorance or stubbornness, but from the body's need for respect. Just as in education there is something in a human being that wants to preserve its natural innocence, so in medicine there is something that doesn't want to subject itself to the machinery of treatment. This thing, this Daphne spirit, is a face of the soul and deserves attention.

I don't mean that the doctor should withhold treatment, but that he could acknowledge a valid and meaningful resistance that serves a purpose. I learned this lesson in home-schooling my daughter in her high-school years. Whenever I became Apollonic in my own need to educate, she drifted away. It's the same pattern in medicine. Especially when the professional gets on a high horse and wants to insist on his expertise or insists that he knows what's good for the patient, he will likely run into the Daphne complex.

Respect comes from deep in the heart, and that is both an advantage and a difficulty. The advantage is that you can come to respect yourself and others, body and soul, by discovering certain truths about life and developing new values. The difficulty is that respect is hard to teach in an academic setting or in a workshop or lecture. Certain things you learn through painful but deepening experiences.

Doctors and nurses may have to cut through attitudes they pick up in a largely technical and materialistic medical education. Much of what they are taught in modernist medicine makes for disrespect. Of course, medical schools don't plan on teaching disrespect for the body, but, as we have seen, leaving out soul and spirit leads to a profound and unconscious failure to respect the physical world, including the human body.

"Respect the Body" could be one of those three-word slogans to keep in mind during all forms of diagnosis and treatment. A patient has to remember this advice as well. Above all, respect your body. If ever you lose that respect and treat your body as an object, you will suffer a loss of soul, and nothing could be worse for your health.

PART IV

PATIENT HEALERS

*It is much more important to know
what sort of a patient has a disease
than what sort of a disease a patient has.*

— WILLIAM OSIER

CHAPTER 13

HEALED
BY ILLNESS

I was in my mid-40s and was living in a small village in the Berkshires of western Massachusetts. The next-door neighbors had just built a house. I developed a strange sharp pain on the side of my chest and my doctor never figured out what it was. At the same time the woman next door felt a similar pain, and we often compared our experiences. Years later I found out that my pain was probably pneumonia, although my doctor treated me for some kind of arthritis. Peg, my neighbor, found out she had lung cancer.

She went a little out of her mind going from doctor to doctor looking for a cure. She lost her personality and wasn't the same at all. She became frenzied. But one day I was sitting in my office with a psychotherapy client when Peg burst through the door. Ignoring the man with me, she shouted out, "I'm healed." She smiled and laughed and looked happy.

"I don't understand," I said.

"I'm going to die pretty soon," she replied. "But I'm healed. I'm okay. I'm better than I have ever been in my life. I'm healed."

From that day, Peg was herself again, perhaps even more so. She was calm and helped her family prepare for her death. I have often seen people go through a similar series of phases: shock, a mad search for a cure, and then acceptance. More than that, the illness does something positive for them. They find strength and a depth they have never had before. People are sometimes healed by their illness.

This phenomenon, becoming more of a person through sickness, presents an alternative way of looking at illness and offers health-care workers a positive challenge in their jobs: to help people go through illness rather than conquer it.

Several years ago a superb East Coast physician asked me to support his book called *The War on Pain*. I thought that this man's work was excellent and his approach to medicine extraordinary. I can't overstate how much I admired him. But I asked him if there was any way he could change the title. I thought, and still think, that the war metaphor takes us down the wrong path.

Here the Tao Te Ching, the unsurpassable source of wisdom from Chinese Taoism, offers clear guidance:

> Accomplish something,
> But not with violence.
> After using force you will lose your strength.
> The Tao doesn't work this way.
> If you go against the Tao
> You will be undone.

But of course it's in human nature to respond to a challenge by reaching for weapons and starting a war, whether you bomb a country or battle drug abuse and cancer. The alternative is not to see illness as an enemy. We all get sick and, most of the time, recover. Maybe we take something from the experience. Maybe we are affected so subtly that we couldn't express what has happened to us. Illness is part of life. You can't improve on life, but you can learn to move more gracefully with it and allow it its ways. You can do this even when you dedicate your life, as my medical researcher friend did, to save people from pain.

How do patients become persons through their illness? In countless ways. They are forced to stop the frenzy of their hyperactive lives. They may be compelled to think and in their own way meditate. That is what I mean by "incubation." Ruminating on their illness, or just having the time to stew, incubates the soul.

Seriously ill people may reconsider what is important in their lives, and they may rediscover the value of the people around them. They may come to the end of hope and learn all over again to pray, to reach beyond their own resources and connect once again with the infinitude of life.

They may value their time on earth as they have never done before. They may make resolutions and plans and reimagine their future. They don't have to change entirely, but they may find a new point of view and a fresh sense of values. The pain in sickness affects the imagination and takes you to places you would not otherwise visit. The depression of being pulled out of life and reminded of your limits and your mortality brings you back into the human race. It's humbling.

Some patients learn through their difficult emotions in times of sickness and through their pain how important it is for them to be with others in their illness. It happens all the time. Patients become aides and volunteers and, sometimes, doctors. In my own experience, students and patients have been inspired by their treatments to become therapists.

Illness can teach and can serve as an initiation, as we have already seen. But this capacity of sickness to be a spiritual passage is not automatic. Many people get sick and demand a pill or a surgery to return to normal as soon as possible. They don't want anything to change. Health-care workers want to make people normal and healthy. They may not see their role as that of a priest initiating a person into the mysteries of life and thereby helping him or her become more of a person.

It's curious that Asklepios for the Greeks was the god not of health but of medicine. Health was the domain of a goddess, Hygeia, from whom we get our word *hygiene*. She often accompanied Asklepios, but she had her own role. Today we make the distinction between medical treatment and wellness centers, understanding that to treat an illness is different from maintaining a state of well-being.

Jungian terms come to mind here. *Animus* is the masculine, spirited, controlling, intellectual, and technical realm, and *anima* is the feminine, poetic, reflective, artistic, and cooperative side. This is a simplification, but it's clear that Asklepios is an animus way of dealing with illness and Hygeia the anima of treatment. Both are useful and necessary.

These two dimensions are a bit like Taoism's yin and yang. Let's refer once again to the Tao Te Ching:

> You do almost nothing
> Until you achieve not-doing.
> When you do nothing, you leave nothing undone.
> The world finds its way when you let things be.
> Chaos results from your interference.

Sometimes doctors and nurses split anima and animus between them, the doctors usually taking on the style of animus. Occasionally you come across a doctor who is full of anima, as I think are many of the doctors today who write about the soul in medicine. Sometimes you find a very animus-style nurse. Once in a while you find both doctors and nurses who have an enviable blend of the two. But typically doctors are in charge and nurses are involved with their patients.

Going through an illness as a rite of passage doesn't mean being passive. A good doctor or nurse could be aggressive in treatment and at the same time cognizant of the value of non-action. Yin and yang are not as literal as they are sometimes imagined. An attitude of strength and skill, coupled with the ability to observe and allow healing to take place, can be part of any doctor's method over a range of temperaments and styles. You adapt the anima and animus or yin and yang to your vision and way of working. Of course, applying these subtle notions to everyday practice isn't as simple as that. It requires years of reflection and attention to oneself, an inner education, to achieve what is not a balance but a reconciliation of the two. A thoughtful reading of the Tao Te Ching would be a good beginning.

How to Be Healed by Your Illness

Let's consider the patient's point of view. How do you deal with your illness as a rite of passage, an initiation? First, you don't have to do much, if anything. When you learn of an illness or first suspect symptoms, your emotions and thoughts will probably go into motion. When my friend John Moriarty was diagnosed with cancer, he reacted the way many people do. He called me and said, "Tom, I've been given a death sentence." When I first learned for certain that I had a blocked artery, I, too, felt considerable anxiety. My thoughts turned to my family. I didn't want to disturb them with the news. I wondered how the children would get along without me.

First, your imagination is flooded with thoughts. Then you entertain these thoughts and give them some attention. I don't mean that you feed your anxiety but that you find ways to express your inner experience. You can do it for yourself by not quickly dismissing these thoughts as negative or troubling. Of course you are going to have troubling thoughts and images at the first sign of illness. You can admit them into your awareness and even give yourself time to reflect on them.

Next, you can write them down in a diary. If you have the slightest inclination toward expressing yourself in words, an illness is a good opportunity for self-reflection. You can also use other forms of expression—poetry, drawing, painting, sculpture, or music. You can have substantive conversations with family members and friends. Conversation is one of the best methods of soul-making. You can even do what Anatole Broyard did to wonderful effect—write a book about your experience of illness and treatment.

While anxiety serves a purpose, it may not be good to remain in an anxious state. It's bad for your health and healing, and it doesn't help with your relationships and reflections. You could find calm in meditation or even a form of yoga suited to your situation and condition. My wife, a seasoned Kundalini yoga instructor, tells me that some of her students are blind, deaf, and wheelchair-bound, and yet they get real benefits from yoga. I myself find that music is an effective tonic for anxiety. Choose your music carefully and really listen to it. Don't use it only as background.

Prayer is another source of deep comfort in the face of serious illness. People often think of prayer in limited ways, perhaps only as petition, asking to be relieved of the suffering and worry. That kind of prayer is appropriate and valuable, but there are other kinds as well. You can pray in gratitude for the life you have had and for the people in it. You can praise life for its beauty and its complexity, for the very mystery by which illness is part of life. You can pray in an open-ended fashion, not asking for anything nor doing anything other than standing at the edge of your existence and affirming life. You can follow the example of Jesus and say, "Not my wishes but yours." Or take what the Buddha has to offer, swallowing the medicine that the Buddha holds in his hand—teachings about suffering and compassion. Or make a simple, spontaneous prayer: "I offer myself to the Mother Earth who gave me my life and who will take me back."

To hospitals I recommend that they make an especially beautiful and calming room where patients can recollect their feelings and thoughts and connect to the infinite source of their lives. The room could have several spiritual resources—books, images, occasional rituals.

Visiting the beautiful but unusual Rothko Chapel in Houston, a place where the focus is a few stark, mainly black paintings by Mark Rothko in an otherwise traditional chapel setting, I noticed prayer books from several traditions available for visitors. Good art can create a potent place for reflection, one that is positive and inspiring and open to a wide variety of opinions and ideas.

I would like to see a shrine of some kind in each patient's room, one that he or she could select as appropriate and that would give daily focus to the profundity of the experience of illness. Patients need spiritual technology equal to the potent materialistic technology that fills hospitals. You have to know in your bones that you're in a place of complete healing and not only bodily treatment. Then you have a better chance of being healed thoroughly by your illness.

While writing this book, one day I walked across the street to say hello to my neighbors and met Jennifer Field, who was visiting them. In 1992, the year *Care of the Soul* was published, she was driving her car a few miles from where I live when she skidded on black ice and plowed into a huge truck. She was seriously injured and just barely escaped death. But she was left with a brain injury that kept her in a long coma, made her largely paralyzed, and in particular caused her to lose her capacity for language and speech.

With the strong support of her mother, she went through a few special kinds of treatment over several years. She had been a prizewinning equestrian, but she had to give up horses. She studied art history, slowly relearned her language skills, and eventually created a one-person show and film about her experience. Her story contains many of the values I present in this book, and her film and show represent a perfect example of how to allow your illness to become a positive strength. Toward the end of her film Jennifer makes an elegant statement that, in my language, well expresses the soul in illness: "My accident has been a positive force . . . It has changed me in ways I will be eternally grateful for."

Jennifer is not stuck on sadness over what she has lost. She understands that now she has new life and new possibilities. Among them, she can use her experience of recovery to help and inspire others. Through her accident she has found a more meaningful life and work than, she believes, she would otherwise have had.

Doctors and Nurses Healed by Illness

I mentioned before the idea of an archetype of healer/patient. This is a pattern wedged deep in the psyches of both people, a pattern that might best be contained tightly in the relationship and in each person rather than split between the individuals. In other words, as we've already seen, it is better for the patient to be part of the healing and the doctor not to be identified as one who doesn't get sick. Yet this split pattern is common. The doctor acts as if he never gets sick, and you would never know by looking at the patient that he has enjoyed a healthy, active life for many years and decades or that he might have some expertise about his own illness.

At an obvious level, the doctor may feel healed when his patient survives and thrives after a serious illness. Before that outcome he may go through an emotional tunnel with the patient, participating in the initiation. This involvement may seem risky, and he or she may look for protection. But the process is part of the calling and allows the doctor to be fully engaged in his profession. Ultimately it is to his benefit. Even if the doctor loses a patient, his openhearted participation places him fully in the arena of healing. The so-called failures are part of the process, necessary to it, taking him down into the lower dimensions of healing, the negative region, so that when he succeeds he will not enjoy a mere egotistical reward but a gift of soul.

As he treats patient after patient, being fully engaged, watching some patients get better and others die or deteriorate, he is taking the risks that make for a deep-seated experience of his profession. He could cheat. He could avoid involvement, excuse his failures, and blame everyone else, including the patient. But this defense against the challenge of his calling weakens his career and will ultimately make him depressed and unfulfilled.

Suicide among doctors is much more common than it is in the general population, and female doctors have a remarkably high rate. Doctors also have a high rate of drug addiction. I've already mentioned that half of doctors interviewed want to quit their profession. We can look for reasons behind these drastic statistics in the cost of malpractice insurance, the impact of managed care, and so on, but ultimately suicide and addiction are due to a weakening of soul—the loss of desire, satisfaction, and purpose.

When any profession collapses in addiction or suicide, we look for concrete, specific, and literal causes. But the onset of problems like these is due to a more philosophical and even theological cause. People lose a sense of meaning and value. Their lives lack purpose and direction. The very things they expected to give them meaning are revealed to be empty. Patients don't appreciate you. They die. Your methods fail. In short, life is more complicated than you expected.

Doctors are not educated in the complexities of meaning. They come out of school with simplistic philosophical ideas. People will love them and appreciate them for what they do. They will be highly respected members of society. They will be rewarded with prestige, honor, and money.

What is absent here is an awareness of soul. A calling to medicine offers profound satisfactions of meaning and respect, but, as I was told often in my hospital visits, many young doctors today focus on the monetary rewards. As a doctor or nurse, you can choose: do you want the respect of your patients and your community, or do you want the materialistic measures of success—bank account, possessions, and prestige? If you are lucky, you will get both. But money is often a substitute for soul values, and if it is the chief motivator, soul may suffer.

Doctors should be the healthiest among us not because they know hygiene, but because they have been healed over and over by their patients. Their patients have taught them courage, hope, and resilience. They have taught them not to give up, how to remain lively and cheerful in the direst circumstances, and how to love and pray and be calm in the midst of profound threat to their very existence.

But for this healing to take place, a health-care worker has to reconcile the split archetype and be open to learning and being healed even as he or she practices medicine. It also requires a level of vulnerability, the thoughtfulness to see lessons when they appear, and the flexibility to change and not remain stuck in hardened positions.

People often talk about the wounded healer, the helper who knows what it's like to be hurt and in need. But there is also the "healed healer," the doctor who by witnessing the courage and deep humanity of his patients has become more of a person himself.

CHAPTER 14

NURTURING THE SOUL

Much of my work in the medical field has focused on helping doctors, nurses, and hospice workers remain inspired in their careers and care for themselves with special attention because of the demands of their work. Patients, too, need to take care of their souls, because, with some exceptions, the health-care system is set up to care for bodies but not souls and spirits. In those areas, for the most part, you're on your own.

My approach to this important matter is simple. I make a list of the things that in general nurture the soul and spirit and then see how they apply in the medical world. My list follows on the next page.

A word about the list: It's artificial and misleading to separate soul things from spirit things cleanly. Usually, and in the best of circumstances, the two are difficult to distinguish and shouldn't be separated. Each person might make a different list, and in fact I encourage you to make your own list before we go on.

SOUL	SPIRIT
Friends	Contemplation
Nature	Nature
Home	Travel
Marriage	Solitude
Beauty	Understanding
Food	Education
Vacation	Retreat
Family	Community
Art	Books
Restaurant	Chapel

Both health-care professionals and patients need to care for their souls and spirits in an environment that is not usually conducive to it. Let's look at the lists and see how a few items might apply.

Friendship. I've been reading literature on the soul for decades now, and I've noticed that friendship is almost always listed as the first priority in caring for the soul. My mentor in this area, Marsilio Ficino, wrote extensively about friends, as have other spiritual writers from antiquity to the present. Friendship is something we take for granted and often underestimate.

Professionals can make friends at work and among patients, and patients can foster friendship with their health-care providers and with fellow patients. These friendships don't have to be profound or bleed out into other areas of life. You can have hospital friendships, passing friendships, professional friendships, workplace friendships. To the soul, what is important is not the length or intensity of the relationship but the quality of the experience of friendship itself.

Sometimes we think of a friendship being good if it lasts a long time. But a brief friendship can be precious and can offer its own rewards. The soul feeds on the sensation of friendship rather than the literal relationship.

Nature. Being out in nature or somehow experiencing the natural world is good for both soul and spirit, in different ways. Insofar as we are part of nature, being in nature is like being intimate with your roots. You see patterns in nature that you feel within yourself—nights and days, seasons, gardens and wilderness, animals and plants. The classical theologians said that we humans have an animal soul and a vegetable soul. You sense this strongly in illness, when your body manifests pathology that seems to have nothing to do with your mind and heart.

You not only find yourself in nature, you can transcend yourself, realizing that the world is infinitely more vast and complicated than your little world. This expansion of vision offers perspective and calm at a time when anxieties are focused on a small portion of existence. A Zen friend once sent me a photograph of galaxies in the sky with the comment: "How can we worry so much about the latest political crisis?"

Vacation. Like friendship, a vacation need not be taken literally as going away for two weeks or a month. Taking a vacation from work and from worry about illness helps the soul. The word *vacation* is from the Latin *vacuus*, meaning "emptied out." We need regular moments of emptying so as not to be overwhelmed by our concerns. Those moments can be days and months or hours and minutes. "Taking a break" is important business.

Medieval and Renaissance writers went further. They said that when you allow yourself *vacatio*, you're separating from the physical world of the body and allowing the soul to come to the foreground. They used examples like sleep, ecstasy, melancholy, dream, and solitude as examples of a soul vacation. The remarkable Romanian Renaissance scholar Ioan Couliano put it this way: "The state of *vacatio* is characterized by a labile link between soul and body which allows it to neglect its physical matrix in order, in some way, better to attend to its own business."[29] Ficino wrote, "Whoever achieved something great in any noble art did it mostly when he withdrew from the body and fled to the citadel of the Soul." He added a line that I have often used on this theme: "The more the external act is relaxed, the more the internal one is strengthened."[30]

Because we are a work-oriented society—we believe that work is virtuous and play optional—we don't understand the deeper value of emptying out of daily efforts and concerns. There is talk of reducing or even eliminating recess and summer vacation from school. Often at work managers merely tolerate breaks and don't do much to make them appealing and comfortable. Doctors and nurses need breaks and vacations like they need continuing education. Patients, too, need distractions from their suffering and worry.

Norman Cousins, the author of *Anatomy of an Illness,* whom I mentioned earlier, wrote about how he watched comedy films when he was in the hospital, and he believed they cured him. I wonder if it was not only the comedy but the break from worry and effort at healing that helped him. He wrote, "I made the joyous discovery that ten minutes of genuine belly laughter had an anesthetic effect and would give me at least two hours of pain-free sleep."[31]

A more exalted way of understanding vacation in this soul and spirit sense is to enter a meditative state in which you unite with the very source of life and have something of a mystical experience. This is a vast issue, each person needing his or her own kind of mystical experiences to keep the spiritual life vibrant.

There is a kind of vacating where you just sit and empty yourself. You become open to life, free of your agendas and interpretations and concerns, taking it all in and being refreshed. You can go deeper and stand at the edge of your world, reaching into the infinite and the transcendent. Many people feel that mysticism is only for specially called men and women, but it is an aspect of the spiritual life that is available to all. It need not be esoteric and excessively complicated. You may have a genuine mystical experience contemplating a night sky.

Beauty. *Nurture* is a good word for what certain experiences in life do for the soul. The human soul needs to be fed on certain kinds of experience regularly, and then it hums along without complaint. But if it lacks certain of these qualities, it can become depressed, lifeless, angry, addicted, and inappropriately infatuated.

With our habit of thinking mechanistically, we assume that when we get depressed or burned out, something must be broken. So we look for the breakdown. We don't usually imagine the problem to be one of failed nourishment. Not knowing much about the soul, because it isn't discussed much in our day, we don't even know what to look for.

You can always count on the soul's need for beauty. An experience of the beautiful can heal many problems. Imagine that you're driving to work and see a spectacular sunrise or just a clear blue sky. You'll probably mention it to someone because it has struck you. In today's world, you get on with life and dismiss the charm you just felt and get back into normal life. Instead, you could cultivate a life of beauty and feed your soul intentionally and regularly, especially when you're sick.

Beauty might be in nature, architecture, sound, painting, photography, colors, or an especially good-looking man or woman. Beauty may be simple or complicated. You probably don't have to argue over the beauty of a sunrise, but a painting? That is open for discussion. Your idea of what is beautiful depends on your experience, education, and background. The old saying is always applicable: "I don't know much about art, but I know what I like."

I happen to have a very strong attraction to the music of Igor Stravinsky. I don't meet many who do, even among my musician friends. I grew up at a certain moment in history and studied music composition when Stravinsky was alive. He also had a love of ritual and spiritual devotion that he put into his music. I can't imagine a more perfect experience of the beautiful than listening to his *Mass* or *Requiem Canticles* or *Symphony of Psalms.*

Beauty vacates the soul, in the way Ficino described vacation. It allows for a mystical union with life and the world around you and sometimes with people. It is a little like Norman Cousins's comedy: it offers temporary relief from worry and pain. But it also brings you close to the sublime, which is the region of the divine.

A book could be written about each of these nutrients for soul and spirit. These examples should point in a certain direction; they offer clues to how we might bring soul to the medical environment and care for our own souls in relation to illness, whether we are patients or health-care givers.

Self-Analysis

Another useful way to take care of your soul is to learn more about the psychology of everyday life. Hospitals and medical centers and clinics are rife with personality conflicts and tensions that could be eased with a little psychological knowledge. Patients carry tensions with their spouses and family members that get in the way of full healing. Books on psychology make it all look impossibly complicated and subtle. People often give up trying to understand their own passions and their relationships.

I have been a psychotherapist for over 30 years, and I've dealt with every imaginable kind of problem and every level of intensity. I don't think that the human psyche is too complicated for an average person to learn enough to enjoy fulfilling relationships at work or at home. Yet I see basic ignorance, even among highly educated medical professionals, about emotions, fantasies, and relationship entanglements.

I was in a hospital once when a nurse in the cardiology unit called the pastoral-care department and said, "I have a patient who needs to talk to someone."

The pastoral person said, "Does she want a priest or a rabbi or an imam?"

"She just wants someone to talk to," the nurse replied.

"I could send a social worker up."

"No. She doesn't need a social worker. She needs someone to talk to."

I thought it was a strange yet typical situation. We are so used to specialization that even when we're just looking for someone to talk to a patient, we can't figure out who is best suited to it.

For one thing, I was disappointed that the nurse herself couldn't have a brief conversation and care for the soul of the patient. She probably didn't think it was part of her job description or within her expertise. Maybe she didn't feel that she had the time. Nor did I understand why anyone in pastoral care couldn't talk to any patient. Do they always have to work by brand—Catholic, Protestant, Jewish? The very idea of needing a specialist for this request seemed odd.

For professionals who need to know a little about simple, everyday counseling, I'd recommend a brief study of Carl Rogers's client-centered therapy. You won't become a professional counselor this way, but you will learn the basics for talking to patients.

As for self-analysis, let me offer this one-page course:

1. Know the key areas in your personality and life where you are neurotic. We're all neurotic, so don't feel bad about it. Don't try to get rid of your neurotic tendencies. Track their history— in your own life and your family. Don't blame

anyone, including yourself. The point is to get to know these neuroses so they don't always do their dirty work from a place of hiding.

Suppose you are insecure in the presence of other professionals. Just know that everyone is insecure at times, even those people who don't show it. When did you start acting this way? Is it part of your family style? Could you admit to it and talk about it with a friend? Could you catch yourself doing it and say to anyone, "There I go being a bit insecure again"? Always admit to who you are, but always have a positive outlook about yourself.

2. In relation to other people, try to do these two things at once: One, be strong, be yourself, say what you think, don't overprotect, don't manipulate. Two, also step back and let others be strong, let them be present as who they are and not who you want them to be, listen to what they say, don't be manipulated.

In general, it's important to do more than one thing at a time. For instance, hospitals revolve around hierarchies of management, surgeons, finance officers, nurses, and so on. These hierarchies create tensions, but you don't have to get rid of them altogether. You can keep a form of management and understand that in any society human beings aren't all at the same level of income, power, and prestige. On the other hand, you can connect with others outside of the hierarchies. You can relate as human beings and talk about things you have in common. We have discussed ad nauseam how doctors can do this with patients, but workers in a medical setting can also do it with each other.

I've been in groups of politicians looking for an elusive common ground. It never appears. But their common humanity is always there. That is a basis for connection.

The same is true in the medical realm. Often there is little common ground between patient and doctor or surgeon and hospice worker. But you do have your common humanity, and you can meet on that high plane. Soul between people is to be found in humor, shared experiences like the weather, physical complaints, food, time, children, and sports. Usually the soul is stirred more by such mundane connections than through insightful and intelligent remarks.

Often what harms relationships is a lack of patience and tolerance, perhaps of forgiveness. People make mistakes. They have blind spots. They say and do the wrong things because something in them bends them in that direction. We all do. These are the complexes, the various neurotic habits that stem from emotional wounds and points of immaturity.

A person who is jealous, for example, is someone who hasn't learned yet how to have someone in his life without possessing him or her like an object. It's fine to feel some prideful ownership of someone, but only if it is complemented with a magnanimous allowance of that person's individuality and freedom. A little jealousy can be a natural and useful emotion that rises up from a desire to have an exclusive place in the heart of another person. It becomes negative and dangerous when it turns into a complex, a habit of behavior that shifts from prideful ownership to aggressive possessiveness.

The jealous person has to mature and soften his claim on a person with soulful understanding that we all have to be free and individual. An immature person doesn't understand this paradox and therefore may become intensely jealous. The word *jealous* is closely related to *zealot*.

Envy, which appears commonly in medical circles, is similar to jealousy. An envious person has not allowed herself to have her own life and to do the things she wants. She sees someone who has given himself these options, and she longs for that freedom herself. In hospitals staff members envy one another's position, promotion, salary, reputation, and opportunities. A patient in a hospital may feel over-whelming envy for visitors and staff who are not sick.

Like jealousy, envy is a sign that a person hasn't learned certain basic lessons in life. The envious one is probably naïve about what it takes to have what you want. She may assume that the person she envies has a perfect life and didn't have to work hard to get where he is. Also like jeal-ousy, envy is the emotion of the one who envies. This state-ment may sound obvious, but envious and jealous people often put all the emotion and blame onto the other person. They don't recognize that their envy is the problem. You are the one with the emotions and it's up to you to become more sophisticated about human relationships.

Earlier, in discussing the qualities of a healer, I referred to self-confrontation, the capacity to ask difficult questions about the way you are. Most of us are good at analyzing others but have many blind spots about ourselves. This capacity to look at oneself, instead of finding fault in oth-ers, helps relationships at all levels. It is one of the most difficult things to do, because it is so satisfying to blame someone else. Blame keeps the pressure off you and defends against self-awareness.

Admittedly, there is pain in self-confrontation. In my own experience, it involves confusion, impatience, and self-criticism that may easily turn into masochistic self-blame. But the rewards of acknowledging your own neuroses are great. Getting through the issues is like making a passage to a new level of understanding and experience.

People also carry grudges and remember offenses and find it difficult to forgive and forget. An important part of mature human relating is the capacity to let go of angry and hurt feelings. Sometimes it helps to remember that you, too, offend people when you don't intend to. Self-confrontation. Or you can just stop, take a deep breath, and tell yourself to let go of whatever is poisoning a relationship.

You will never get along with some people. Personalities do clash. In that case you can do your best to be civil and limit contact if possible. Sometimes people are put together who will never find peace between them. That is where the manager comes into play. A nurse manager or a hospital human-relations officer or a vice president of staff who is psychologically aware and astute can help keep personality problems from corroding the staff.

A final resource for being more psychologically mature in a medical setting is civility. Civility is a quality in a person and in human exchanges in which simple forms of respect, some formal and some informal, give an encounter a foundation for contributing to the common good. When people hear the mention of civility, they often recoil because they are so sensitive to the shadow of civility—artificiality, insincerity, and covering over real emotions. But, while these shadow qualities threaten to weaken the power of civility, they don't completely take it away. Using language and gestures of respect lays the groundwork for good working relationships. Civility doesn't require intimacy or profound feelings. The point is to take care of basics and then build on them.

Today we seem to be in a worldwide culture of decadence. Politics is crude, the media have no limits on sexual expression and violence, and people talk to each other with little, if any, respect. Road rage has its counterparts in workplace rage and living-room rage. Americans still operate with the pioneer or survivalist spirit and often don't trust formality and reserve.

Medicine takes part in this dip in civil discourse. Receptionists treat you like an object and get annoyed with your failure to understand the language and rituals of the medical culture. Nurses deal with you as though you hardly exist as a person. Doctors look bored or impatient as you discuss life-and-death issues with them. Simple civility would go a long way in preventing much confusion and hurt among patients.

Patients treat health-care givers in the same way, demanding too much, being quick to criticize and compare and impatient to be served. Maybe it would help to have rules of civility posted in hospital hallways and patients' rooms.

One day I was walking through Saint Francis Hospital with Bill Priftis, a hypnotist who works within the integrative-medicine department. Bill's main purpose is to help relieve anxiety in patients who are dealing with a host of challenges. Bill presents himself well and is a model of civility. I followed him on his rounds and watched how he treated everyone with extraordinary respect. At each patient room he would stand at the door and ask to come in. He would explain who he was and what he had to offer. Politely, Bill would ask the patient if he could do anything, and then, with permission, he would speak kindly and softly, leading the patient to less agitated breathing and to a place of general calm.

On one floor, Bill had to ask at the nurse's station for the room number of a patient who had requested his services. A senior nurse walked by.

"Who is this?" she asked another nurse.

"He's a hypnotist from Integrative Medicine," the other nurse said.

The senior nurse rolled her eyes and said, "Great, a hypnotist."

All this took place in the presence of Bill and me. I wondered why this nurse, who clearly had authority and prestige on her unit, couldn't gather up a little civility and treat Bill better, whatever she thought about his work and however ignorant she was of the contribution hypnotists can bring to medical practice. I understand that hypnotists have a difficult time in general with the very name, and some are using other terms for what they do. But the lack of civility rang out in that encounter.

Being civil is not the same as communicating genuinely at a deep level. It is the foundation for more intimate connection and allows a community to operate effectively and pleasurably. It can be taught and fostered by a management team that understands and appreciates it.

One day I went to see a doctor, who had his practice in a hospital I was visiting, for a personal physical complaint. I had an appointment at opening time and went to the glass window to say that I had arrived. The receptionist growled at me saying that she needed my insurance card and needed it quickly. When I produced an out-of-state card she didn't recognize, she was not happy. When I finally saw the doctor, he examined me briefly and gave an opinion. No hello, no "Glad to see you," no assurances, no nontechnical recommendations. Just 15 seconds of simple, caring conversation would have made me feel much better about seeing this man. I appreciated his expertise, but I don't know if he has a soul. I certainly didn't see any signs of it.

On the other hand, once a year I go to a dermatologist for a checkup. We have a warm and friendly meeting, even though I'm fully unclothed and he's seeing several people in each appointment hour. We always chat about something and shake hands coming and going. He does an expert job, as far as I can see, looking for signs of skin cancer. This man's soul shines through on his face. It's my assumption that he enjoys his work, because he looks and acts like a man who takes pride in his medical ability. I look forward to the once-a-year 15-minute meeting.

The word *civility* comes from the Latin *civis*, a citizen, a member of the community, and ultimately goes back to the idea of "home." To be civil is not to be a friend, a lover, or a family member, but to be a fellow citizen. You treat people as members of your community, not as strangers, and certainly not as objects. The feeling of home and community lies in the background of civility.

A doctor, a nurse, and even a patient are all doing the work of citizens, because in a community we care for each other. Teachers teach, police officers protect, and doctors and nurses heal. In this community we are all also patients and have an opportunity to be civil to those who take care of us.

Care of the soul is not psychoanalysis. You don't have to examine yourself and your history and figure yourself out. It's all about care in your everyday life. Care for your home, your family, your children, and the people you encounter. It is not heroic, but it requires attention. The implication for the way we are as doctors, nurses, and patients is quite evident. You go about your work with care and treat people with respect. There are no deep psychological issues involved. There is nothing to lose and little to risk. Yet, after spending some years observing medical teaching and practice in several countries, I am convinced that these two simple virtues could transform health care and contribute to the health and well-being of patients everywhere: care and respect.

CHAPTER 15

A PRACTICAL GUIDE FOR PATIENTS

Those many years ago when I was in a hospital in Northern Ireland for an appendectomy, I was on a men's ward that had a dozen beds at least, as I remember. One night I was going off to sleep. The lights were out, and the hospital was quiet. Suddenly a voice whispered into my ear: "What kind of ice cream do you like?" Two of the patients on the ward were getting ready to raid the kitchen.

It helps to understand that a head nurse, called Sister, who behaved much like a commanding officer in the military, managed our wing of the hospital. She was to be feared and obeyed. The day a tall old man on the ward, whose feet stuck out past the end of the bed, screamed loudly for his staff, meaning his cane, or when a young orderly gave him his bedpan upside down, she was not amused. So I wondered at the daring of my comrades who were determined to raid the kitchen in the middle of the night. But raid it they did. Within a half-hour they wheeled a noisy stainless-steel cart into our ward, teeming with many different varieties of dessert and tea.

I have other warm memories of that hospital stay: waking from the anesthesia to behold two hairy, knobby knees at my bedside—my surgeon wore kilts. One day two ancient Catholic sisters came to my bed. They said they had relics of a saint that they wanted to press on my wound. They inserted their slender fingers under the sheets and groped about, searching for my lower-abdominal sutures. Living in a religious community and under the vow of chastity, I fell in love for a week with a kind, rosy-cheeked nurse who protected me from the matron. On the whole, there were many soulful moments during that ten-day hospitalization.

Decades later I spent a day and a night in a Boston hospital for a heart procedure. It was an uneventful stay—no hefty matrons, nothing to laugh at, no late-night raids, and no one to fall momentarily in love with. Of course, I was there for a short time. The staff seemed to expect me to watch television throughout my stay. I tried to get the large old television high on the wall at the foot of my bed working, but later someone told me that it was defunct, even though I had a remote at the bedside. Instead I was told that I could order up a movie or check my e-mail on the computer next to the bed. One catch: I couldn't get up to go the closet for a credit card. No one appeared in my room for hours, so I practiced zazen.

Differences in time and place separate these two hospitals, but it is clear that the earlier, Irish experience was more soulful than the latter. Sometimes you see the soul of a place more in its mess than in its order. The Boston hospital was neat and ordered, but it was also sterile, at least for me.

Be an Individual

Once again, remember Aristotle: The soul is what makes you uniquely who you are. To keep your soul in the medical world, preserve your individuality. When they talk about you as a case, remind them who you are. When they forget your name or simply don't use it, make a point to state it loud and clear. If possible, wear clothes that overstate your individuality and compensate for the tendency to make you look like all the other patients. Make your room a statement about who you are and what you like.

You can bring something of home to the hospital: photos, throws, pillows, paintings, statues, rugs, and a mirror. Hospitals restrict the use of mirrors, which makes one wonder if there isn't some potency there. So smuggle in a little mirror and something else that is forbidden. To preserve your individuality, you may have to bend the rules, because the rules are there to keep the place emotionally cool.

If people want to bring you flowers, ask for dramatic ones, anything that will make you and your space individual. If anyone complains, tell them you are only doing what Aristotle recommended.

Color is important, too. Color is a symbol of life, and yet whenever people begin to describe a hospital, the first thing they talk about is the bland color. You probably can't paint your room, but you can bring in fabrics and objects that splash some color around an otherwise dull space.

All of this symbolism I learned from Marsilio Ficino, who said that your choice of color, images, sounds, and textures invites different "spirits" into your world. It is not a matter of mere décor but of powerful influences that may or may not foster your healing.

If you express your soul, you will be eccentric. There is no other way. You will rub people the wrong way. They will criticize you. They may be uncomfortable with your individuality. Most people prefer conformity and homogeneity. Heterogeneity is threatening. An institution usually prefers that everyone fade into the background of acquiescence. The organization runs better when people stifle their spirits and camouflage their souls.

There is something inherently aggressive about expressing your individuality. You stick out. You poke the status quo. You refuse to adapt. You upset whatever equilibrium has been achieved.

But from your point of view, this assertive individuality is life and vitality, which are important in reestablishing health. Remember that Asklepios, the spirit of healing, was a snake. He was not a domesticated animal, though he liked the company of his dog. A snake is threatening, and yet it is the very symbol of healing and medicine.

Hygeia, health, was shown in sacred sculpture feeding a snake from a cup that she held in her hand. She was nurturing, perhaps, but also intrepid, a friend to the chthonic beast, the snake that often lies hidden on the earth. You might think that her animal would be a lamb or a cow, something more obviously nurturing and friendly. But no, health is a snake. To be healthy is to be like a snake. Remember this when you see the snake all over the hospital as a symbol of medicine.

To be healthy, you nurture your deep and hidden serpent-like feelings, tend your hidden past, and feed your deep desires. People are often afraid of their desires, thinking that they will lead them into dark and objectionable places. But desire always leads onward toward something of merit. There is an interesting and profound relationship between the erotic life and health.

See the Eros in Medicine

The word *eros* is a stumbling block to many a modern reader. I once gave a lecture to a group of business leaders about eros and leadership, and afterward they complained to me for using such a salacious word. But I have studied Greek literature, where Eros is a divine spirit responsible for creating a beautiful and cohesive world, and my use of *eros* is positive. Eros is the force responsible for both objects and people coming together in creative forms of union. Eros keeps the planets in orbit and people united.

In the *Symposium,* Plato's tale of a party of speeches in which eros is praised, eros is described as a healing force. It unites what was once separated. The sexual connotations of eros have to do with this power to unite and draw together. People are attracted sexually, of course, but eros also allows their worlds to overlap and intertwine. Eros makes marriages and communities, orgies and societies.

Eros embraces the realm of pleasure, joy, union, attraction, beauty, and desire. It is healing because it draws together what has been kept apart or what has fallen apart, even body elements. Doctors follow eros when they seek their specific careers and look for the right place to set up practice. Nurses pursue eros when they go to the bedsides of patients and linger there and do the job they take pleasure in. Even patients observe the laws of eros when they seek the healing person or place for their illness. Apparently, illness needs a sexual companion.

It is no accident that television shows about hospitals are filled with erotic attractions, mainly among the healthcare workers. But it is widely known that patients often fall in love with their doctors and nurses. Communities often gather around their hospitals to support them, in a grand erotic gathering of lovers and patrons.

Classical literature distinguishes the various kinds of love: family, friendship, sexual, and communal. Eros is both cosmic—the planets staying on course—and deeply personal. Eros is the passionate desire that keeps you alive and draws you into the future.

In sickness, eros can grow weak. You may feel like giving up. You feel defeated by an illness you didn't want and can't control. Yet eros is the sensation of being alive and is therefore important and helpful for getting better. I see eros in Norman Cousins responding to his life-threatening illness with humor. I see eros in Anatole Broyard dealing with his fatal cancer with wit and sharp analysis.

I see eros in the memory of my mother, a few weeks before dementia set in, sitting in her wheelchair, waiting for her granddaughter to arrive, wearing a smart scarlet sweater over gray flannel slacks, her hair combed carefully over the scar of her brain surgery. It took great effort from her to look bright and, she would say, presentable to her granddaughter. Whatever in her didn't want her granddaughter to see her disheveled by her illness was an erotic spark keeping her in life.

This kind of eros, so simple and virtuous, invites soul into a hospital or sickroom and contributes to the healing, if not to the cure, of the disease. How helpful it would be if doctors and nurses were aware of its importance and would help their patients foster it in the many small ways available to them.

A central ingredient in eros is pleasure. Epicurus, the philosopher who taught that pleasure is a primary value in every life, specifically said that during illness even a small quantity of pleasure preserves your humanity. In his famous Letter to Idomeneus, written literally on his deathbed, he wrote about the effect of the soul's pleasure at a time of physical pain: "I write this to you while experiencing a blessedly happy day, and at the same time the last day of my life. Urinary blockages and dysenteric discomforts afflict me which could not be surpassed for their intensity. But against all these things are ranged the joy in my soul produced by the recollection of the discussions we have had."[32]

This is the Epicurean philosophy, which any medical center could adopt: in the midst of bodily pain, how important is the pleasure of a conversation with a friend, or even the memory and the story of such a conversation. In other words, no matter how pressing the physical pain may be, don't neglect the soul's pleasures, which can have a healing effect.

Epicurus said something else applicable to medicine and illness: "Just as there is no benefit in medicine if it does not drive out bodily diseases, so there is no benefit in philosophy if it does not drive out the disease of the soul."[33] I have used this statement for years as an inspiration to think of theory and ideas as therapeutic, but the statement can be turned around to suggest that ideas and reflection can cure the soul.

A hospital or medical center can be a place of ideas as well as treatment. It could sponsor lectures and events that are not explicitly medical but rather touch the soul with depth of insight. Earlier I described my visit to the Planetree hospital in Derby, Connecticut. I was surprised and delighted to see how they had placed their library just off the entrance to the hospital, and they did this intentionally, understanding how important ideas and books are for the sick and for health-care workers. True, the emphasis there seemed to be on technical research, but it wouldn't take much to include philosophical ideas and spiritual explorations into disease and treatment. This emphasis would add a valuable Epicurean touch to medical knowledge, professional and amateur, and in that way would include the soul.

With Epicurus in the background, a patient might appreciate visits and letters from friends as part of the healing. He could welcome such visits and make an effort toward hospitality. He could make some phone calls and write some notes, if he's up to it, and take the initiative in caring for his soul in an Epicurean manner, focusing on deep friendships and simple pleasures.

There is an effective rule about caring for the soul that I learned from my studies in Renaissance practice: small means produce the best result. That means that the slightest gesture to include soul can have an effect far beyond its size. Put a flower in a tiny vase on your food tray and notice the transformation.

In my visits to hospitals for this book, I toured kitchens and spoke to food-service managers. Many of them would like to make a patient's experience of food beautiful and humane, but they don't have the resources. They have to provide a bare-bones service simply because of the budget. That means that you, the patient, must take the opportunity to add some grace to your eating. When people bring you flowers, you can ask them to get you a small vase and then you can cut a flower for each meal. You can bring a single cup or plate from home that you find beautiful. Then you will have given your soul two things it needs—beauty and a piece of home.

Be Your Own Spiritual Guide

Although the spiritual life is about the infinite and the invisible, about mysteries and the unfathomable, we know from religions and spiritual traditions around the world that it is also full of ritual, symbol, prayer, literature, music, and contemplation. In your own small way, you, the patient, can create a spiritual atmosphere around your illness and healing, whether you are in the hospital or at home.

In the West, generally we have not taught or encouraged people to be spiritually creative. We want them to follow their leaders like sheep massing behind the shepherd. I am always uneasy when I hear a minister or priest refer to his people as his "flock." In the East, people revere their traditions and know them quite well and yet use their imaginations to create home and personal rituals. There need be no conflict between personal piety and traditional belief.

A sick person could give himself a half-hour of solitude every day to be quiet and contemplative. Where the Zen master tells you to "sit," you can "lie" in your bed for a set time of contemplation. I say contemplation because you may or may not meditate in a formal way. If you have a habit of meditating, of course it would be appropriate to meditate in bed or in a chair. If you don't meditate formally, you can still give yourself a set time to be quiet and undisturbed. The quiet itself is the goal—a calming of life around you and a quieting of your thoughts and emotions.

If you are seriously ill, prayer may come to you automatically. You may ask for a cure or an easing of pain or just the ability to handle the illness. But no matter how serious your illness, you may also benefit from prayers in your religious tradition or in another tradition. Even if you're not religious, traditional prayers may give you a language that offers you some peace and hope.

Hospitals and medical centers, even doctors' offices, could provide books or leaflets of prayer from a variety of traditions. The impulse not to force any religious belief on patients is important, but it is not necessary to create a completely secular environment. The obvious middle way is to draw on many different traditions, including nondenominational forms, to calm, inspire, and connect illness and healing to the infinite.

Here, for example, is a prayer from the Upanishads:

> The Lord of Love hides deep in the heart
> Of every being, finer than the most refined,
> Greater than the most immense. Through his gracious power
> You leave behind your selfish needs and despair
> And become one with the World's Soul.[34]

Or this passage from the Irish prayer "Saint Patrick's Breastplate":

> For my protection today I summon:
> The power of the sky
> The brightness of the sun
> The paleness of the moon
> The glare of fire

The speed of the wind
The depth of the ocean
The firmness of the earth
The steadiness of a rock.[35]

These prayers are full of devotion and yet should not offend any modern person's sensibilities. The Irish prayer seems particularly potent to me because, when I am faced with something seriously threatening, I look to nature for permanence and hope. If the sun and moon are on schedule, everything else is in order.

In the age of the iPod and other personal music players, you can keep a playlist of spiritual music or music for healing, to be used in doctors' offices and in the hospital. Music has the extraordinary power to move you in ways that words can't touch. Rather than listen to anything that is available for patients in the hospital system, off-the-rack music compilations, it might be better to be thoughtful in making your own, subdividing them for ease of use when you are in situations where music might help.

In the golden age of soul, when Ficino was teaching how to make a soulful personal life and society, he specifically recommended care in selecting music. He himself played different kinds of music for people depending on their needs of the moment. He used astrology as a model for this music therapy—Venusian music to charm, Saturnine music to deepen, Marsian music for strength, and so on.

We don't have to use the astrological model literally, but it does offer an example of how we might choose our music for the spirit it creates and the impact it has on our emotions and thoughts. We could think specifically about needs when we are sick and give music a place of importance in our healing process. A hospital could help by providing the technical means for using music as part of individual healing. You don't have to make obvious selections, but you could think it through carefully and make precise compilations, drawing from a wide variety of sources and styles. I might put Willie Nelson next to Bach, for example.

In times of healing, most people need calming music, something to deal with their anxieties. Chant, the sounds of nature, and the old standard songs work for many. Some hospitals offer live music from local musicians, and that has special power to transform the environment. Hospitals are also experimenting with music in operating rooms, although problems of taste and loudness come up among staff and patients.

Be Part of a Community

The notion that a human person is a complicated being encased in a body is entirely wrong. Jung once wrote that "the soul is for the most part outside us." A human person is someone linked to other persons at various levels of intimacy and intensity. It is the soul that offers the possibility of linkage, and to bring soul into the healing process requires the constant and close involvement of others.

As a patient, therefore, you can invite those close to you to participate in your illness. You can talk to them about it openly and invite them to be with you at those times that are most appropriate. People often don't know whether to give you privacy or offer you companionship. You can help by showing them clearly what you would like and when you would like it. Hospitals and their staffs could help by welcoming family and friends to be involved as much as possible. Of course, you don't want them getting in the way, and of course a patient needs privacy and solitude in certain measures. But the presence of relatives and friends is essential to the healing process.

Community is also part of the experience. There are those at a distance who are concerned about you and want to help. You can invite them by informing them of your progress and thanking them for their attentions. When my friend James Hillman had serious surgery to remove a tumor from his lung, his wife, Margot, kept his community informed by means of occasional e-mails that were welcoming, warm, and full of gratitude. It meant a great deal to those of us at a distance to be included, and I know it was important to James. He said so many times.

If you could sit in on staff discussions with nurses, doctors, and various attendants, you, the patient, would realize that those people who care for you daily are also involved in your welfare. They are not mere functionaries. A word of thanks or a sign of affection means a great deal to them and in fact allows them to continue with their challenging work. They are part of the community that defines who you are when you are sick. Perhaps if you saw them as such, they would learn to take that role more seriously in their work with you.

Doing research for this book, I have had the opportunity to observe from behind the scenes. Patients surely don't know how involved nurses and doctors can be in their illness and recovery. Nurses and doctors talked of their habit of phoning in to work to see how a patient was doing.

My impression is that hospital staff members are for the most part deeply engaged with patients, but because of overwork and the demands of paperwork they are always in a rush and may slight their patients inadvertently.

Some people not in actual contact with patients nevertheless feel involved. I was talking with a woman who had been working in the corporate world and recently took a job raising money for a hospital. "I feel that my life now has added meaning," she said. "I'm doing something for people. Even though I rarely see patients, I am helping them deal with medical challenges, and that gives meaning to my life."

It's easy to use words like *meaning* and *help*, but when people say that working in the health field has this dimension, they are speaking from their hearts. It makes all the difference to be making a living by helping people deal with illness and accident. This is work that is qualitatively different from another kind of work and creates a special kind of community. A patient is part of that community. Maybe that is why former patients often want to work in a health field or, if they have the means, offer financial support.

There is some argument over whether health care is a right or a privilege. Another way to imagine the issue is to understand that a human community offers certain things to its members: education, protection, and healing foremost.

Community is not just a collection of people, but a spirit of common concern and need. It's impossible and undesirable to go it alone in this world because we need what others give us. We are essentially communal, and it is that spirit that accounts for a patient's respect and gratitude for a health-care worker and the doctor's or nurse's satisfaction in doing the work. Because community arises from such a deep necessity in a person, it is a major source of soul in the medical realm.

In hospitals, a breakdown in community often comes from the tendency of specialists to focus on themselves. One part of a hospital will not know what another part is doing. I ask someone in brain trauma about a new development in the oncology unit and he knows nothing about it. Patients, too, may be isolated in their rooms or units and experience the hospital in a very small way.

There are television and computer screens everywhere, in all waiting rooms and in each patient's room. I can imagine the patient being offered presentations about the hospital so that he would have a better idea of where he is and what is going on around him. Staff not related to his case could say hello, in passing, and just offer a word or two about what they are doing. Solutions to soul loss are usually quite simple.

One hospital my wife visited had bingo games once a week that boosted the sense of community in a remarkable way. At Saint Francis, potential financial donors were invited to tour the hospital wearing white jacket and nametags, as though they were doctors on the staff. This inspired idea lets us know how breaking the barriers helps community. Saint Francis wanted the benefactors to feel more part of the hospital, but why not do the same for everyone connected to the hospital life—not necessarily dressing the same, but breaking through the layers of prestige and the class system?

Dr. Baxter describes how, at the Bronx AIDS hospital, patients in extreme need helped each other cope and created a feeling of community among themselves and with the staff. Sometimes this development was minimal: "It was difficult to pinpoint exactly when Rosa's soul began to resurface from her private underworld, but rumblings were detected sometime between the second and third week of her hospitalization. Perhaps it was the first time she found her meal not to her liking and did not push it onto the floor, instead simply opting to complain about it to her nurse. Or maybe it was the first time she held the door open for a housekeeper struggling to take his mopping bucket out of her room."[36]

Small signs of a communal feeling—an opening of the heart, if only a narrow gap—show that a person has a soul. Patients could acknowledge this by greeting each other and refusing to be isolated. Health-care workers could also break out of the glass cage of their professionalism to generate community. It doesn't take much.

Find an Advocate and Navigator

In one of the greatest pieces of world literature, Dante has a moment of sleepy disregard and finds himself in the underworld, where he sees many extraordinary sights that disturb and inspire him. Fortunately, he meets up with the Italian poet Virgil, who serves as his guide. As Anatole Broyard said, we all need a Virgil, especially when we enter the underworld of illness.

Just as community is an archetypal pattern in human life, not just an external organization, so having a guide during times of challenge is also archetypal, profound in its meaning and emotion. During illness we need family and friends and can benefit from community wherever we can find it. We also need a guide to help us sort out issues of symptom, meaning, and treatment. In the complex world of medicine and at a time of personal weakness, it helps to have someone who can speak for us, get the information we need, and plead our case.

Often a family member comes forward, someone who knows the world of medicine or has a talent for dealing with its complexity and its habit of withholding information and support. Sometimes it's a member of the medical team who singles you out as a person he wants to assist in a special way. When I was in my teens, a dentist discovered that I had a badly impacted tooth and required oral surgery. At that time a dental intern was connected to our school in some way and became interested in me and my mouth. He guided me through the entire process, standing next to me as the surgery took place and following up with me in the weeks of healing. I've never forgotten his kindness, which calmed me and colored the event with the warm hue of friendship.

Today some nurses have the official position of navigator, helping patients deal with the foreign world of medical treatment. In some hospitals the role of nurse-navigator is institutional and bureaucratic, but in most situations it is a very human position in which the cool hospital meets the warm needs of a patient and his family.

The job description of a nurse-navigator may be technical and organizational, but in practice the role is usually intimate. The navigator helps explain conditions and treatments and acts as a link to doctors and specialists, but she also offers comfort and companionship to patients, especially in crucial times of worry and confusion.

In the absence of a nurse-navigator, a chaplain or pastoral counselor may help. When my mother had her stroke, I went first to the chaplain at the hospital and received information and advocacy. Without the continuing help of this chaplain, who was a Catholic sister, I don't know how we could have managed.

I have also found that friends who are doctors have all been extraordinarily generous with their help explaining treatments and medications, and sometimes they make telephone calls to other doctors as advocates and "Virgils."

The navigator/advocate is a soul companion, someone who stands in front of you at a time of crisis or weakness and fights the battles and learns the secret codes. At the conference on health literacy I mentioned, a film was shown of various people talking about their medications. A kind middle-aged man was taking a drug for hypertension, but when the interviewer asked him what hypertension was, he had a mistaken notion that it just meant "being hyper, excited." He didn't know that he was being treated for high blood pressure. That man needed an advocate, and the point of the film was that many patients don't understand their conditions, treatments, and medications. Sometimes they need an interpreter for the arcane language used by pharmacology and medicine in general.

Nurse-navigators are occasionally former patients who know the illness firsthand and yet also have the medical training to deal with hospitals and doctors. These are special kinds of Virgils, people who can carry on their own healing through helping others deal with an illness they know intimately. In a way, this is the perfect resolution of the patient/healer split. Their intimate knowledge of the illness also brings soul to the relationship.

Caring for Your Soul as a Patient

A patient in the medical system cares for his or her soul by coming into it as a full person, a person with a body, soul, and spirit. He has the presence of mind not to enter the unconscious mythology by which illness is seen mainly as a mechanical malfunction of a body part. He knows that every second of his life, including a time of illness, he is a person with a history, a family, friends, work, a home, and a world of meaning and values. None of these things can be set aside just to focus on healing a part, as though the patient were an automobile in for servicing.

The patient does his best to connect with the people who are caring for him, even if they seem to be focused only on the technical aspects of their jobs. He includes his family and friends, keeping them informed and inviting them to participate, with necessary limits. He gets the right combination of solitude and social interaction that he needs—we all have different tastes in this area. He brings beauty into his environment according to his own taste and abilities. He is friendly and does what he can to strengthen the spirit of community around him. He offers hope to himself and his family through clear and appropriate spiritual ideas, language, and practices.

A person with soul has a sense of humor, wit, and intellect. He doesn't offer himself without reservation to the system, nor does he constantly complain and carp. He acknowledges his fears and hopes and helps those around him heal and be comfortable.

The shadow side of being a patient is also part of the soul. That may include anger, depression, frustration, impatience, hopelessness, and sentimentality. The patient with a soul allows these things without letting them dominate. During the treatment of a significant illness, you not only go through a process of physical healing, you also endure a rite of passage in which you mature emotionally, intellectually, and spiritually. A thoughtful person allows this change to happen and appreciates how certain strong emotions are part of the process.

It may be necessary to be angry at life that it has given you this challenge. I think of my friend John Moriarty, so full of life and hopes for the future and yet overwhelmed by a heavy attack of cancer. He seemed to be surprised and outraged that life would cut him short. But, as I have already indicated, he changed. Eventually he came to see that human beings get sick and die in the middle of their precious plans and hopes, something he knew in theory but never had to confront.

After going through intense emotional ups and downs, John changed, and at his death he was a man at peace. It does indeed seem that we may go through phases in an illness. I don't think the phases are the same for everyone or for any one person over the course of different illnesses. I don't want to limit or predict what a person will experience. But we might expect a variety of unpredictable developments.

Fear, begging to be released, anger, and even denial may all serve a purpose in the final engagement with an illness. It is usually assumed that denial is sheer avoidance of the pain and mortality in a serious illness, but it could just as well represent a desire for life. Even if it is rooted in fear, we may have to acknowledge and feel our fear fully before we can go on to another, more positive attitude.

When a person like John feels that he's been delivered a death sentence, those around him could give him some slack, some time to find a way to cope. If he has to deny, that is fine. It's only human. Behind our expectations to react maturely and sensibly lie hidden a moralism and perfectionism that is deeply embedded in our culture. We could be quicker to forgive and understand.

Medicine especially has an annoying tendency toward moralism. I was once traveling in Europe with my family when a bill came in from a doctor who had been treating my daughter. As soon as we got home, we sorted through the bills and found that this one was overdue. But before we could pay it, we received a phone call from the doctor's office from an irate and offended bookkeeper who lectured us on the high reputation of the doctor and then told us that if we missed another payment we could no longer see him.

According to one psychological rule, when we lose sight of a precious and sacred quality, it doesn't disappear but takes a superficial and corrupted form. We saw this rule implicit in the role of the doctor's receptionist. Once, she would have had the sacred duty of protecting the holy mysteries. Today, she has the pseudo-sacred position of guarding the secrets of the physician's office. Similarly, the bookkeeper in my story treated the doctor as though he had a sacred position, but "sacred" here didn't mean truly spiritual, just inflated.

Moralism is a corruption of a refined ethical sense. Of course, I should pay my bills on time, even if I'm away in another country. But I could work out an arrangement with the doctor rather than be scolded, warned, and threatened. This kind of moralism creeps into many exalted cultural institutions—education is another—but it is common in medicine.

Forgiveness in its many forms is a better alternative to moralism. The medical establishment might go a long way toward gaining soul if it were more accepting of human imperfection and the struggle to deal with mortality and the mysteries of medical treatment.

CHAPTER 16

THE SOULFUL DOCTOR AND NURSE

In this book I am writing to both patients and health-care workers. I don't split these roles because it helps if doctors and nurses remain in touch with their vulnerability and patients in touch with their powers of healing. When roles get separated too far, power issues become dangerously volatile and the healing process turns into mere treatment. How, then, can the health-care worker bring soul into his practice of medicine?

We have seen many ways in which medicine can change to open the way for the deep soul. Now perhaps we can look more specifically at the education and work of the health-care specialist. As always, we look back at the basics of the soulful life and apply them to the profession of medicine.

An Education in Healing

Let's start from the beginning—education. In medical school, is the purpose to train a doctor for the job of

treating illness or doing research, or is it to create an educated person who has a deep understanding of illness in the
context of an individual and of society?

Let's consider the words we use. In English, we refer to
a doctor and automatically think of a physician. But we use
doctor for advanced degrees in many fields. I am a doctor
of religion. The word comes from the Latin *doctus*, which
means "educated." Cicero, one of the highest authorities
on Latin usage, speaks of a person educated (*doctus*) in the
humanities and in Latin.

Other languages speak of a healer, as in the Italian
medico and Spanish *médico*. But we also have the German
Doktor. There is a plus side to the word *doctor:* A doctor is
someone who is educated and cultured and at the same time
technically skilled to promote healing. Throughout the
history of medicine, worldwide, we find this combination:
a broad educated vision coupled to technical know-how.
The ancient Greeks educated a person in the sciences and
humanities for both personal excellence and good citizen-
ship. They called it *paideia. Doctus* or *doctor* could be a good
translation of the Greek ideal of paideia, a person broadly
and deeply educated for active and intelligent participation
in community.

The great 16th-century physician Paracelsus adds
important ingredients: He wrote extensively about the education of a physician, again pointing out the two dimensions: becoming both a cultured and a highly trained
person. He also stressed the motive of the real physician:
love for humankind. He said that a real doctor has a single
focus—persons in distress. He also said that a doctor must
appreciate the spiritual source of his calling and ability. His
own words are powerful: "The physician should address
things that are invisible. What is visible should be part
of his knowledge, and he should recognize illnesses, just
as those who are not physicians can recognize them, by

their symptoms. But this doesn't make him a physician; he becomes a physician only when he is knowledgeable about the unnamed, the invisible, and the immaterial factors that play a role."[37]

A doctor, as distinct from a technician, has technical skills and intuitive abilities in relation to the body all nestled within a broad education in culture. To be accurate with our words, it might be better to speak of "medical specialists" rather than "doctors" when discussing the students we generally turn out of medical schools.

In my visits with residents—doctors getting further knowledge and experience—I had one frequent experience. I would talk about the role of spirituality and even theology in matters of medicine, suggesting the need for a broader education, and they would look at me with alarm. Why? Because they have so much to learn at the technical level, they couldn't imagine getting a broader education as well.

Another problem is a lack of understanding of the liberal arts. Once, I was standing in line at a university bookstore when two business students in front of me were talking about buying books in literature. "How is this going to help me make a deal?" one was saying to the other. "Beats me. It's a waste of time and money."

I can imagine a doctor saying, "How is Shakespeare going to help me perform surgery?" The answer is that the practice of medicine will become more and more dehumanized and depersonalized the more technically it is imagined. The arts and humanities, including my field of religious studies, help a person explore and sort out ideas about ethics, responsibilities toward community, the meaning of a human life in the face of mortality, and so on. These are crucial issues that every patient and his family faces and on which physicians notoriously stumble. The lack of a liberal-arts education shows in the face of every nurse and doctor who looks helpless when a patient's family asks him for hope.

Paideia, becoming a cultured person, would also help a doctor or nurse do challenging work without burning out, getting depressed, turning cold, finding relationships impossible, and having no reserve or resources for his or her own well-being. A liberal-arts education makes life interesting and valuable. From it, education draws much of its soul.

Is there a doctor in the house? Only if a person is *doctus,* educated, cultured, and possessing vision and taste. In the history of ancient Greece, philosophy grew up with or perhaps out of medical exploration and discussion. Today you meet doctors who can talk about art, literature, and society intelligently, because there is a mysterious, profound connection between healing the body and developing the soul. The body is the soul, after all, according to William Blake.

Paracelsus says that a real doctor knows the invisible issues at work in illness. A contemporary modern physician might take that to mean bacteria, tumors, and genetic faults. Paracelsus no doubt was talking about theological matters and mysterious patterns and developments that can be known only symbolically, say, by studying the stars and planets.

You can also know the invisible matters through the arts. Although the argument about religion and art, especially art as religion, has gone on for centuries, I have no doubt that art serves the spiritual life. This is especially so when art has a place at the center of culture, but that can only happen when a culture has learned how to be religious and spiritual without losing its precious secularity. We have not yet been able to achieve that goal satisfactorily.

A doctor or nurse who has some sensitivity to art and for whom art plays a significant role in life has contemplated the deep issues that always come up in the medical arena. Illness makes for good theater, as we know from many television hospital dramas, and for good literature and visual art. Art attempts to express the inexpressible, conveying both suggestions of meaning and the mysterious elements that can never be known fully.

Illness is similar: you can explain it to a point, but then the mysterious takes over. Why this person and not the one next to him or his brother? Why did it appear now in life? What was its cause? Is there poison in the air he breathes or in the way he lives?

The Soul Doctor

Our idea of the doctor as doctus, one who has truly been educated, given the paideia that makes him or her a person of special character and keenness of mind and imagination, can take us out of the dark age of modernism. It can restore an idea of the physician and the nurse as people of vision and personal brilliance and taste.

To become a person rather than a mere individual in the unconscious mass of humanity, you need to know the secrets of the natural world, including the human body, and the secrets of meaning that only the arts can offer honestly, and the secret of emerging from the profound narcissism in which, as Freud said, we are all born. That is, by being exposed to the great spiritual teachings of the world we can rise up out of unconsciousness and stop reacting blindly to our individual and social challenges. We can sculpt a vision of what a mature human being is like and can make steady progress toward that goal. As the ultimate achievement, we can become pliant, contributing members of the local and global community.

This kind of person, much in the pattern of Paracelsus, knows the wide world and therefore can practice medical skills with wisdom and humanity. He doesn't reduce human experience, including illness, to the physical body, but understands that issues of soul and spirit play themselves out in our illness and therefore have an important role in healing. He is not a stranger to the religious and spiritual issues of humanity. He is not ignorant of the role of emotion and fantasy in sickness and healing.

Months before his death from cancer, Anatole Broyard wrote, "I would like a doctor who is not only a talented physician, but a bit of a metaphysician, too. Someone who can treat body and soul. . . . My ideal doctor would 'read' my poetry, my literature. He would see that my sickness has purified me, weakening my worst parts and strengthening the best."[38]

But how do you prepare a man or woman to be such a doctor? He or she has to have explored the deepest, most common questions of soul and spirit. What does it mean to read someone's poetry? To see meaning in illness, in the way person deals with adversity, in the nature of the family that gathers around? To ask the poetic, spiritual questions about the specific illness? Has your lung cancer anything to say about the way you breathe in and breathe out the world?

Remember Susan Sontag's reservations about this approach. "Nothing is more punitive than to give a disease a meaning—that meaning being invariably a moralistic one."[39] Yes, it's true that we sometimes blame people for doing something that brought on their illness. "You ate too much fat. You didn't exercise. You didn't express your anger." And people can be made to feel guilty for the sin of getting sick. But it's going too far to say that all efforts to find meaning in illness are moralistic. It is certainly possible to explore a connection between the way we live and the way we get sick without blame. It is a matter of self-analysis, not self-accusation.

Dr. Baxter looks at the ruined lives of the people under his care and sees reason for bliss rather than blame. He tells the story of a physician's assistant from Peru who worked with him assisting HIV patients. The health-care worker himself was sick, and one day, Pedro fell into a coma. Dr. Baxter began asking himself uneasy questions about whether he had given enough attention to Pedro. He knew that Pedro was a mysterious sort who didn't reveal much about himself, but he also remembered one small item—"He always offered to share his snacks with me and the other ward staff, and he would often buy treats for his patients."[40] Dr. Baxter concludes that Pedro was generous and bighearted. He is reading his colleague's poetry and finding humanity in it.

I sometimes wish a doctor treating me might see something of who I am and not just my malfunctioning body parts. Sometimes doctors ask questions but don't even listen to my answers. I had a family doctor for several years who guided me through some complex medical issues. He never called me by my name, and he never said a word that wasn't about diagnosis and treatment. Maybe it was his personality, but I always felt that there was some underlying tension in his work.

I haven't found this clinical detachment much among nurses. The difference between the groups is so clear that I came to understand that the psyche of a doctor is generally far different from that of a nurse. Perhaps the doctor takes too much responsibility for the well-being of his patients. A nurse is usually involved and engaged personally with her patients, while a doctor is more distant and guilty about any setbacks. This could be the shadow side of wanting to have too much power of life and death and not allowing for fate, God, or the gods as they dish out destiny. Dr. Baxter is always saying that he has to lighten up and stop blaming himself for every problem that arises among his patients, and this is a doctor with extraordinary self-knowledge and vision.

I'd like to teach a counseling psychology/spirituality course to doctors. It could be a brief course in learning how to listen and speak effectively to patients and other staff members. It could offer a philosophy of illness that includes family members and the whole of a patient's life.

It could help the doctor be inspired about his or her calling and see its spiritual dimensions. It could help the doctor learn ways of caring for his own life—his home, marriage, children, body, and friends. It could offer a brief self-analysis, so that the doctor would not be so unconscious about how human beings operate emotionally and spiritually and what his own issues are. It would offer resources in the arts and spiritual literature that might enrich his life and that of his patients.

I'd also like to write a pamphlet for patients, reminding them that for a human being there is no such thing as a soulless, spiritless body. It is artificial in the extreme to imagine and then treat the body as a purely physical set of organs modeled on a machine. I'd invite them to nurture their sensitivity to themselves as complex beings—body, soul, and spirit—through all sorts of treatments and examinations that assume a body without a history, relationships, and meaning. I'd suggest that they include their families and friends intimately in their treatment, that they bring some objects from home to warm up their hospital rooms, that they dine when it is time to eat, and that they pray before important tests and procedures. I'd recommend putting images of healers nearby—famous or favorite doctors; Jesus, the Buddha, or Quan Yin; or a family member known for holiness or empathy.

When I sat with Ira, the man I mentioned who had cancer and heart problems, about seven nurses came and went in his room, checking EKG reports, blood pressure, and pulse, showing considerable concern, and mentioning several times that the cardiologist would be coming to make final decisions. No one told Ira what was wrong, and he was reticent to ask questions. He joked frequently, but his humor seemed to cover over his anxiety and frustration. In my pamphlet I would encourage patients to have a family member or friend nearby in such situations or, if possible, to ask direct questions themselves instead of being left in anxious limbo.

Cultural Transformation

Many groups of nurses I spoke with in the research phase of this book told stories of frustration and anger over doctors and hospital administrators who fail them in two ways: they have not yet absorbed the fact that nurses today are professionals with advanced education and specialized skills, and they stick to an old-fashioned hierarchical system of authority and power. The nurses hope for the day when they will be able to influence decisions and have a voice. Meanwhile, they are patient, as the hoped-for shift in the culture of medicine slowly comes into place.

Traditions, hierarchical organization, and respect for personalities have given medicine a rich, deep culture, but they have also created rigidity, sexism, and authoritarianism. In medical meetings and in encounters between patients and doctors, the air is often thick with the theatrics of prestige and power. Doctors are at a level below the angels but above the normal human being because of their specialized knowledge, skill with care of the body, and everyday dealings with life and death. Many physicians are not able to separate the office from the person, so they identify with the office, acting as though their elevated position is due to their personal qualities rather than their calling. We saw before that the solution to this swelling of ego is to be a big enough person to fit the calling.

Planetree hospitals demonstrate how a much-needed shift in culture can happen. In their case, a hospital is imagined and then designed from the top down to be a culture that is liberated from the unconscious assumptions that rule most medical centers. I visited many hospitals where certain sections or units were reimagining the way they do things, but these groups had to struggle daily against a larger organization dedicated to the old ways. My experiences make me wonder if important changes in medical culture will reach a tipping point only when entire organizations dedicate themselves to a new vision.

Slowly we are moving into a new era. We will eventually live by a new mythology that will offer an alternative to the modern myth that dominated the 20th century. But this shift in meaning and values will take place through hit and miss, error and brilliance. It will not be an advance in culture as a whole, but a movement in every sphere of life, including medicine.

For medicine is not really a science. It is one of the ways human beings use technical knowledge and skills to apply the compassion they have learned through spiritual experiences and education and through a liberal education. Medicine truly belongs among the humanities. Science serves the art of medicine. Technicians have the potential of becoming doctors.

Every time I see a new book written skillfully by a surgeon or other kind of doctor, I'm reminded of this fact that medicine is only secondarily science. Above all, it is a way of being in community with generosity and empathy. When I hear nurses and doctors talk about spending extra unpaid hours at their labors, I'm reminded that the profession of medicine is part of a larger calling to service.

A patient should also be aware that illness is not the same as a malfunction in a machine. When you go to the doctor or enter a hospital, you are not bringing your body parts to be fixed. You are dealing with a profound spiritual issue, the encroachment of your mortality and a gap in the unconscious flow of your existence.

It is a matter of meaning, emotion, relationship, and ongoing engagement with life. Illness is first of all an experience of soul and spirit manifested in the body. Your caretakers are priests and sacristans in the sacred work of healing and caring. You are a devotee, a suppliant of Apollo, Asklepios, Hygeia, the Lapis Lazuli Radiant Healing Buddha, Jesus the healer, and Quan Yin. Even a surgeon applying her skills is only aiding in the work of these deep healers. All healing, including the most technical, is an achievement of the medicine spirit and a matter of the most profound mystery.

ACKNOWLEDGMENTS

Many doctors, nurses, and pastoral counselors have helped me in the research for this book. I couldn't list them all, but I want to single out Saint Francis Hospital and Medical Center in Hartford, Connecticut, for allowing me to explore every corner of the hospital and talk to every staff member who was interested. At Saint Francis my old friend Rev. Marcus McKinney was generous beyond measure in welcoming and hosting me. In the administration of that hospital, the CEO, Christopher Dadlez, and Sister Judy Carey were constant advocates of my work there. The manager of integrative medicine, Sharon O'Brien, made it all happen and brought intelligence and grace to our discussions with the staff.

At the University of Minnesota, I want to thank Dr. Mary Jo Kreitzer and Catherine McLaughlin, and at McGill University Medical School, another old friend and constant supporter, Dr. Balfour Mount, who gave me guidance whenever I asked for it. At the University of Tennessee Medical Center, Rev. George Doebler and Rev. Steve Sexton showed me what spiritual counselors can do for the sick. Steve also gave me some golf tips.

In New Hampshire I have had the support of Peter Gosline, President and CEO of the Monadnock Community

Hospital; Maryanne Mercier, a thoughtful and forward-thinking nurse; and my dear friend Dr. Bettina Peyton. Dr. Susan Frampton, president of Planetree, encouraged my work, even though she works at these values every day. Dr. James Wiggins, in his usual heartfelt and intelligent manner, gave me feedback from his own experiences that confirmed my approach.

I also had warm support from Hay House. First and foremost, Louise Hay and then Reid Tracy supported me in writing what I was inspired to write. Then the backup from Patty Gift and the people behind her gave me confidence. My agent, Kim Witherspoon at Inkwell Management, has been just superb.

During the writing of this book I was homeschooling my daughter, Siobhán, for her high-school years, and she doesn't know how much our discussions influenced me. Hari Kirin always helps me sort out my ideas and plan my projects and serves as resident muse. Her own work as a teacher of yoga instructors and as a painter inspires me every day. Abe, too, a young man with a future, is always in my thoughts as I write.

You'll notice in this book that I write a lot about my parents. I was lucky from birth to have parents whose example guides me in all my work, and particularly in this book on medicine's soul and spirit.

ENDNOTES

1. Allan J. Hamilton, M.D., FACS, *The Scalpel and the Soul* (New York: Jeremy P. Tarcher/Penguin, 2008), 189.

2. Raoul Birnbaum, *The Healing Buddha* (Boston: Shambhala, 1989) 62.

3. "The Physicians' Perspective: Medical Practice in 2008," The Physicians' Foundation, October 2008, www.physiciansfoundations.org/usr_doc/PF_Survey_Report.pdf.

4. Pauline Moffitt Watts, *Nicolaus Cusanus* (Leiden: E. J. Brill, 1982), 39. My translation.

5. Joseph Campbell, *The Hero with a Thousand Faces* (New York: MJF Books, 1949), 82.

6. Laura Stokowski, "The Inhospitable Hospital," *Medscape Nurses,* June 2008, http://cme.medscape.com/viewarticle/574813. Thanks to Maryanne Mercier for alerting me to this fascinating article.

7. Daniel Baxter. M.D., *The Least of These My Brethren* (New York: Harmony Books, 1997), 129.

8. Anatole Broyard, *Intoxicated by My Illness* (New York: Fawcett Columbine, 1992), 35.

9. Mircea Eliade, *Journal III: 1970–1978,* trans. Teresa Lavender Fagan (Chicago: University of Chicago Press, 1989), 211.

10. Mircea Eliade, *Journal I: 1945–1955*, trans. Mac Linscott Ricketts (Chicago: University of Chicago Press, 1973), 108.

11. Broyard, 42.

12. On this point and on the "archetype of the invalid" see Adolf Guggenbühl-Craig, *The Emptied Soul*, trans. Gary V. Hartman (New York: Spring Publications, 1999).

13. Norman Cousins, *Anatomy of an Illness* (New York: Bantam Books, 1981), 160.

14. Charlotte Parker and Virginia Parker, *Return to Joy* (Dallas: Dancing Horse Publishing, 2010).

15. Hamilton, 47.

16. Mark S. Hochberg, M.D., "The Doctor's White Coat—an Historical Perspective," *Virtual Mentor* 9, no. 4 (April 2007): 310–314.

17. Mircea Eliade, *Shamanism* (Princeton: Princeton University Press, 1972), 148.

18. Cindy Sanders, "Looking Good Is Half the Battle," *Nashville Medical News*, http://nashville.medicalnewsinc.com/news.php?viewStory=1012.

19. Åke Hultkrantz, *Shamanic Healing and Ritual Drama* (New York: Crossroad, 1992), 86.

20. John Louis Bonn, S.J., *So Falls the Elm Tree* (New York: Macmillan, 1947).

21. Vincent Scully, *The Earth, the Temple, and the Gods*, rev. ed. (New Haven: Yale University Press, 1979), especially page 206.

22. Pausanias, *Guide to Greece, Volume I*, trans. Peter Levi (New York: Penguin Books, 1971), 194.

23. *Paracelsus: Selected Writings*, ed. Jolande Jacobi, trans. Norbert Guterman (Princeton: Princeton University Press, 1979), 73.

24. Sackett, D. *Evidence-based Medicine - What it is and what it isn't*, 1996, http://www.cebm.net/ebm_is_isnt.asp.

25. Adolf Guggenbühl-Craig, *Power in the Helping Professions,* rev. ed. (New York: Spring Publications, 2009), 94. I strongly recommend this book to anyone in health care. I have used it in my teaching for 20 years.

26. Richard von Krafft-Ebing, M.D., *Psychopathia Sexualis* (New York: Pioneer Press, Inc, 1953), 131.

27. Bernd Jager, "From Medicine to Hypnosis to Psychoanalysis: A Reflection on the Human Body." Privately circulated paper.

28. Robert Moss, *The Secret History of Dreaming* (New York: New World Library, 2009).

29. Ioan P. Couliano, *Eros and Magic in the Renaissance,* trans. Margaret Cook (Chicago: University of Chicago Press, 1987), 49.

30. Quoted in Paul Oskar Kristeller, *The Philosophy of Marsilio Ficino,* trans. Virginia Conant (Gloucester, MA: Peter Smith, 1964), 217.

31. Cousins, *Anatomy of an Illness,* 39.

32. Brad Inwood and L.P. Gerson, eds, *The Epicurus Reader* (Indianapolis: Hackett Publishing Co., 1994), 79

33. Inwood, 99

34. Shvetashvatara Upanishad, III. TM version.

35. TM version.

36. Baxter, *The Least of These My Brethren,* 77.

37. *Paracelsus: Selected Writings,* 63-64. Translation adjusted by TM.

38. Broyard, *Intoxicated by My Illness,* 40, 41.

39. Susan Sontag, *Illness as Metaphor* (New York: Farrar, Straus and Giroux, 1978), 58.

40. Baxter, *The Least of These My Brethren,* 185.

ABOUT THE AUTHOR

Best-selling author and psychotherapist **Thomas Moore** has written numerous books on spirituality, including *Writing in the Sand, Soul Mates, Life at Work,* and the *New York Times* bestseller *Care of the Soul.* Born in Detroit, Michigan, Moore has devoted his life to the study of theology, world religions, Jungian and archetypal psychology, the history of art, and world mythology. He currently lives in New Hampshire.

We hope you enjoyed this Hay House book. If you'd like to receive our online catalog featuring additional information on Hay House books and products, or if you'd like to find out more about the Hay Foundation, please contact:

Hay House, Inc., P.O. Box 5100, Carlsbad, CA 92018-5100
(760) 431-7695 or (800) 654-5126
(760) 431-6948 (fax) or (800) 650-5115 (fax)
www.hayhouse.com® • www.hayfoundation.org

———

Published in Australia by: Hay House Australia Pty. Ltd.,
18/36 Ralph St., Alexandria NSW 2015
Phone: 612-9669-4299 • *Fax:* 612-9669-4144
www.hayhouse.com.au

Published in the United Kingdom by: Hay House UK, Ltd.,
The Sixth Floor, Watson House, 54 Baker Street, London W1U 7BU
Phone: +44 (0)20 3927 7290 • *Fax:* +44 (0)20 3927 7291
www.hayhouse.co.uk

Published in India by: Hay House Publishers India,
Muskaan Complex, Plot No. 3, B-2, Vasant Kunj, New Delhi 110 070
Phone: 91-11-4176-1620 • *Fax:* 91-11-4176-1630
www.hayhouse.co.in

———

Access New Knowledge.
Anytime. Anywhere.

Learn and evolve at your own pace
with the world's leading experts.

www.hayhouseU.com

Printed in the United States
by Baker & Taylor Publisher Services